eat.shop paris 2nd edition

an encapsulated view of the most interesting, inspired and authentic
locally owned eating and shopping establishments in paris, france

researched, photographed and written by jon hart

cabazon books : 2010

table of contents

eat

shop

ion's notes on paris

something sounds too good to be true, I have found it usually is. I don't like being such a skeptic, but I ave heard too many things described as magical and revolutionary when they were simply average and rdinary with a strong marketing team behind them. In this world where so many things are "spun," can nything live up to its hype? Paris does.

lo matter how many times I visit Paris (which has been often over the last two decades), my breath is al-vays taken away while walking through the arcade of trees in the Jardin des Tuileries toward the immense nd phenomenal Louvre. And not even the most flowery of culinary adjectives can make the satisfaction of onsuming an authentic, fresh-from-the-oven *pain aux chocolate* from a top-notch *boulangerie* any better. here is no need to sell Paris using huckster techniques as Paris is simply splendid.

n my experience, the best way to experience Paris is by foot with a metro card in your pocket. When your eet can't take it any more, get on the metro. It is super easy to figure out and will get you anywhere you vant to go, fast. Weekly metro passes are worth it and are valid from Monday to Sunday. For shorter visits *carnet* (book of ten tickets) can be purchased at a discount from automated machines. The same tickets re accepted on the clean and efficient buses, which provide from its large windows one of the best, and heapest, sightseeing tours on earth. I also recommend buying the little red map book, *Paris Classique ar Arrondisement*. It is essential to help navigate all of the tiny streets of this city and can be found at nost tabacs. Make sure to read the "about eat.shop" on the next page for more helpful hints.

n addition to the multitude of wonderful shops and restaurants in this book, here are a few other ways o spend your time:

> *Act Pious*: On Sunday afternoons around 4:30p, hear a free concert courtesy of a giant pipe organ vhile enjoying one of the most magnificent buildings in the world: Notre Dame.

> *Act Worldly*: Go to the Mosquée de Paris and experience the delights of the Arab world. One can njoy the hammam or simply stop by for mint tea > www.la-mosquee.com

> *Act Design-y*: Visit Le Corbusier's Villa La Roche. Built for a collector of avant-garde art, this house s an architectural masterpiece > www.fondationlecorbusier.fr

> *Act Like a Bigwig:* Visit Drouot, the legendary French auction house. There is no cost to watch the uctions of incredible art and antiques; just keep your hand motions to a minimum > www.drouot.com

about eat.shop

• All of the businesses featured in this book are locally owned. In deciding which businesses to fea-
ture, that's our number-one criteria. Then we look for businesses that strike us as utterly authentic and
uniquely conceived, whether they be new or old, chic or funky. And if you were wondering, businesses
don't pay to be featured—that's not our style!

• A note about our maps. They are stylized, meaning they don't show every street. If you'd like a more
detailed map, we have an online map with the indicators of the businesses noted > map.eatshopguides.
com/paris2. While in Paris, make sure to have a detailed map with you like the *Paris Classique Par Arrondisement* found at most tabacs. Because this city has so many tiny streets that sometimes change name
mid block, it's imperative to have this tool.

• Make sure to double check the hours of the business before you go as they often change seasonally.
Also many businesses in Paris close for the month of August, so make sure to call before you go.

• The pictures and descriptions for each business are meant to give a feel for a place. Don't be upset if
what you see or read is no longer available. Many of the food descriptions are in French. If you need help
translating, you can get a translation app for your phone or use Google translate.

• Small local businesses have always had to work that much harder to keep their heads above water. During
these rough economic times, some will close. Does this mean the book is no longer valid? Absolutely not.

• The *eat.shop* clan consists of a small crew of creative types who travel extensively and have dedicated
themselves to great eating and interesting shopping around the world. Our authors write, photograph and
research their own books, and though they sometimes do not live in the city of the book they author, they
draw from a vast network of local sources to deepen the well of information used to create the guides.

• There's a number of great indie, English-language bookstores in Paris. Librairie Galignani, Shakespeare
& Company, The Red Wheelbarrow, Village Voice Bookshop, The Abbey Bookshop and Tea & Tattered
Pages to name a few.

• *eat.shop* supports the *3/50 project* (www.the350project.net) and in honor of it we have begun our own
challenge (please see the back inside cover of this book).

• There are three ranges of prices noted for restaurants. $ = cheap, $$ = medium, $$$ = expensive

previous edition businesses

you own the previous edition of *eat.shop paris*, lucky you. Since it sold out in 2009 it has become highly coveted. So make sure to keep yours. Think of the first edition and this new edition as a "volume" to give complete view of *eat.shop's* Paris. If you don't have the previous edition, make sure to not miss the businesses on this list. They are all amazing.

eat

la mère de famille
angora
u petit fer à cheval
istrot paul bert
ouillon racine
read & roses
afé charbon
afé de l'industrie
afé vavin
hartier
hez casimir
hez prune
tablissements vinicoles
le france
ranterroirs
otel du nord
as du falafel
ecume st-honoré
enclos du temps
os à moelle
a cigale recamier

la palette
le bac a glaces
le bistrot du peintre
le c'amelot
le nemrod
le petit lutetia
le petit vatel
le progrés
le pure café
le rubis
le taxi jaune
le timbre
les cakes de bertrand
marché boulevard raspail
marie quatrehomme
pâtisserie sadaharu aoki
pho banh cuon 14
rose bakery
saint germain crêperie
tesnime
tokyo eat

shop

atypyk
biscuit sec
blackblock
carouche
celis
chône
coquelicot paprika*
cuisinophile
dominique picquier
e. dehillerin
emmanuelle zysman
erotokritos
et puis c'est tout!
58m
gaspard yurkievich
hoses
jouets
bass
l'objet qui parle
la droguerie
lieu commun

liwan
liza korn
m.a. dauliac
magasin sennelier
marché saint-pierre
marie papier
miller et bertaux
ofr*
pages 50/70
patyka
porte de vanve flea market
renhsen
shine
the collection
the lazy dog
tsumori chisato
ultramod
voyages

a previous edition business does not appear on this list, it is either featured again in this edition, as closed or no longer meets our criteria or standards. If it's starred, it has moved.

where to lay your weary head

There are many great places to stay in Paris, but here are a few of my picks:

hôtel amour (9th arr)
8 rue navarin
33 (0) 1 48 78 31 80 / hotel-particulier-montmartre.com
standard double from 140 euros
restaurant and bar: yes
notes: hotel of the moment with marc newsom-designed rooms

hôtel du petit moulin (3rd arr)
29 - 31 rue du poitou
33(0) 1 42 74 10 10 / hotelpetitmoulinparis.com
standard double from 190 euros
restaurant: no bar: yes breakfast: yes (additional fee)
notes: 17th century bakery turned into a stylish christian lacroix-designed hotel

hôtel particulier montmartre (18th arr)
23 avenue junot
33 (0) 1 53 41 81 40 / hotel-particulier-montmartre.com
union double suite from 290 euros
restaurant: no bar: no breakfast: yes (additional fee)
notes: luxurious mansion with garden

hôtel saint vincent paris (7th arr)
5 rue du pré aux clercs
33 (0) 1 42 61 01 51 / hotel-st-vincent.com
standard double from 150 euros
restaurant: no bar: yes breakfast: yes (additional fee)
notes: delightfully serene

haven in paris
617.395.4243 / haveninparis.com
studio apartments start from 750 euros a week up to
4 bedroom apartments from 3500 euros a week
notes: stylish rental apartments

arnaud delmontel

all-around awesome bakery and pastries
39 rue des martyrs. corner of rue navarin. metro 12: notre-dame-de-lorette
33 (0) 1 48 78 29 33 www.arnaud-delmontel.com
wed - mon 7a - 8:30p

opened in 1999. owner / chef: arnaud delmontel
$: visa. mc
lunch. treats. first come, first served

9th arr >

Naming your favorite baguette in Paris is like trying to name your favorite tree in the forest. Still people take a shot. At the top of many a list are the *bâtards* (loafs) at the famed *boulanger* and *patisserie*, *Arnaud Delmontel*. I can concur—these loafs are *la crème de la crème*. I used to live nearby and would often buy my bread here while picking up a few "extras": a flaky caramel and fleur de sel galette one day, a meringue and chocolate fantasy called *Le Vacherin* the next. I began to believe I must visit here daily because it was one-stop shopping. *Très* convenient.

imbibe / devour:
macarons
royal tart
tartelette citron
patte d'ours
campagne raisins
financiers
coeur frivole
millefeuille varié

bistrot mélac

wine-focused bistro

42 rue léon frot. corner of rue emile lepeu. metro 9: charonne
33 (0) 1 43 70 59 27 www.melac.fr
mon - sat noon - 2:30p, 7 - 10:30p

opened in 1938. owner: jacques mélac
$-$$: visa. mc
lunch. dinner. reservations accepted

11th arr >

You never know what you are going to get when you spend an evening at the *bistrot à vins*, *Mélac*. It all depends on who is sharing the room, or sometimes the table, with you. I have had joyous, convivial nights here with a soccer team celebrating the day's win, and cozy rainy nights when another bottle of wine sounded like the perfect antidote to the wet weather. Coming to *Mélac* is like life—sometimes it's raucous and other times not. The consistent part is your mustachioed host Jacques, who is always gracious, his wine key always at the ready.

imbibe / devour:
08 domaine laurens marcillac
07 domaine ballorin et fils les chenevieres
07 domaine morin bourgogne chitry
assiette du fromage
pavé de boeuf avec pommes de terre
roti de veau braisé
plat du marché
pruneaux et fromage blanc

bob's juice bar

a shockingly healthy alternative

15 rue lucien sampaix. corner boulevard de magenta
metro 5: jacques bonsergent
33 (0) 9 50 06 36 18 www.bobsjuicebar.com
juice bar: mon - fri 7:30a - 3p kitchen mon - sat 8a - 3p sat - sun 10a - 4p

opened in 2008. owner: marc grossman
$: visa. mc
breakfast. lunch. first come, first served

10th arr >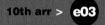

You are never going to guess what the hottest trend in Paris is right now: health food! Made by an American!! *Mon Dieu*!!! Traditionally what has passed for "healthy" in Paris has been a salad weighed down with mounds of ham and Cantal cheese. Then *Bob's Juice Bar* opened on a side street off the Canal St. Martin, offering fresh-squeezed juices and vegetarian dishes. This is a business model that, until recently, sounded akin to opening an air conditioning shop in the arctic. It just goes to show, you can teach an old dog new tricks—as long as it's a veggie dog.

imbibe / devour:
cocktail de jus
100% fruit smoothie
housemade muesli
conscious chocolate
futomaki
tomato cashew nut soup & muffin
quinoa avocado salad
pumpkin sweet potato coconut soup

breizh café

breton crêperie

109 rue vieille du temple. corner of rue du perche. metro 8: saint-sébastien froissart
33 (0) 1 42 72 13 77 www.breizhcafe.com
wed - sun noon - 11p

opened in 2007. owner / chef: bertrand larcher
$-$$: visa. mc
lunch. dinner. first come, first served

3rd arr > **e04**

I know, I know. A crêpe shop in Paris, whodathunkit? Well keep your sardonic criticisms to yourself until you try *Breizh Café*. This is not your normal street vendor selling fluffernutter roll-ups. I'm talking farm-fresh eggs, homemade caramel, fresh butter from Breton, unpasteurized Gruyère. Everything is made fresh from the best ingredients available and served in an extremely pleasant, modern environment. Still haven't convinced you? Dozens of artisanal ciders should be enough to win over even the most jaded of grumps. I know you are sold now. And if you aren't, fine. More for the rest of us.

imbibe / devour:
thé vert
chocolat chaud "maison"
crêpes:
 beurre, yuzu & sucre
 dame tatin
 campagnarde
 paysanne
cancale oysters

café de l'epoque

a classic brasserie

2 rue du bouloi. corner of rue croix des petits champs
metro 1: palais royal- musée du louvre
www.lecafedelepoque.fr 33 (0) 1 42 33 40 70
mon - sun 11:30a - 11p

opened in 1826
$-$$: all major credit cards accepted
lunch. dinner. full bar. reservations accepted

1st arr > **e05**

You won't be without options for a place to rest your weary feet in Paris, so how to choose? Follow my hints to eliminate the not-so-good options. If most of the patrons are reading Rick Steves guides, keep walking. A roving accordionist hovers. Run! The menu indicates all food is on sale. Dud! If you are near the Palais Royale go to one of my fave classics: *Café de l'Epoque*. Not only does it pass all of my tests, but it also offers very good, straight-ahead food and drink. And it's mere yards from the Louboutin shop, handy for catching your breath after dropping 1,000 clams for some new heels.

imbibe / devour:
coca light
poireaux vinaigrette
assiette de sauton foie & toasts
saucisson de lyon & salade lentilles
tartare de boeuf, frites & salade
steak haché à cheval
profiterole chocolat

cafés et thés verlet

coffee beans and drinks

256 rue saint-honoré. between rue saint-anne and rue des pyramides
metro 1: palais royal-musée du louvre
33 (0) 1 42 60 67 39 www.cafesverlet.com
mon - sat 9a - 7p

opened in 1995. owner: eric duchossoy
$: visa. mc
coffee / tea. treats. first come, first served

1st arr >

Let's get one thing straight. Everything is not better in France. In fact, this country has a dirty little secret. The coffee is not that good unless you like it espresso-like (i.e., extremely dark), kind of burnt tasting, and always requiring sugar. But fear not as there's *Cafés et Thés Verlet*. This historic café is a rare gem in Paris. Not only are the exotic coffee beans and teas here sold in bulk chosen for subtlety and complexity, this is also where to get a cup of really good coffee. Though I may sound rigid and pigheaded, like I require my morning frappucino—*au contraire*, a venti mocha works for me too.

imbibe / devour:
coffees:
  australia skybury
  guatemala antigua victory
teas:
  keemun f. o. p.
  golden tips
  mokalbori
vanille noisette

chapon chocolatier

award-winning chocolates

69 rue du bac. near rue de grenelle. metro 12: rue du bac
52 avenue mozart. between rue du ranelagh and rue de l'assomption
metro 9: ranelagh
33 (0) 1 42 22 95 98 www.chocolat-chapon.com
tue - sat 10a - 7:30p

opened in 1986. owner / chocolatier: patrick chapon
$-$$: all major credit cards accepted
treats. first come, first served

7th arr >

Just as I would rather not learn about my friend's sexual fantasies, I don't really want to hear their chocolate fantasies. They have them—I know, because I do, too. At least I do since I learned about the chocolate mousse bar at *Chapon Chocolatier*. Along with the ganaches and pralines is an honest-to-goodness, buy it by the kilo, mousse bar where chocolate is whipped into heavenly suspension with differering intensities. This stuff is so good it makes me want to bring some home, put on my French maid outfit, and... I know, I know, t.m.i.

imbibe / *devour:*
mousses:
  équateur
  sao tome
  madagascar
  cuba
praline with pink berries
lime ganache
coulis de cassis

chauvoncourt

a simple café

22 rue henri monnier. between rue de navarin and rue victor massé
metro 12: pigalle
33 (0) 1 48 78 26 03 www.chauvoncourt.com
mon - sat noon - 3, 5:30 - 11p

opened in 2007. owner: christophe charton
$-$$: visa. mc
lunch. dinner. first come, first served

9th arr > **e08**

Every job has its cross to bear. Mine is having to eat in restaurants around the world. People often offer, "I'll be your assistant." But I know they couldn't handle the pressure. I am a highly trained eating athlete, having built my stamina over the years. Amateurs would crumble under the pressure of successive days of long lunches. Then again, there are times, like at *Chauvoncourt,* when dining is easy with Christophe graciously hosting, delivering his charcuterie along with a whimsical story. OK, this doesn't sound tough, but sometimes it's a hard job. Honest.

imbibe / devour:
06 montepulciano d'abruzzo fonte venna
08 olivier moril bourgogne-chitry cave
porchetta & salade verte
bresaola de boeuf
scamorza grillée & jambon de norcia
soufflé d'artichauts
salade de thon, haricots blancs, céleri & oignons
tiramisu maison

chéri bibi

fun bistro

15 rue andré del sarte. between rue de clignancourt and rue charles nodier
metro 4: chateau rouge
33 (0) 1 42 54 88 96
tue - sat 8p - midnight

opened in 2007. owner: yannig samot
$$: visa. mc
dinner. full bar. reservations recommended

18th arr >  e09

What's more important for a night out: delicious, innovative food or a super fun atmosphere? Depends on the night I'd say. There are times when studying each bite of your meal, like a scientist, is perfectly entertaining. Then there are nights when you want to feel like you've just been to Studio 54. Good news—*Chéri Bibi* will work for both kinds of moods. The menu has verve with new takes on old classics made with confidence and panache. And I doubt the always happening crowd would mind if you stood up and did a few Donna Summer moves after finishing your *plat du jour*.

imbibe / devour:
06 pascal lallement brut reserve
rhum arrangé
la terrine maison au porc & pruneaux
le fromage de tête de chez durard
le pavé de saumon mangues & sésame
les noix de st. jacques
le gâteau tout choco de colette
tiramisu classique á l'amaretto

25

coco & co

all eggs, all the time
11 rue bernard palissy. between rue de rennes and rue du sabot
metro 4: saint-germain-des-prés
33 (0) 1 45 44 02 52 www.cocoandco.fr
mon - sat 10:30a - 5p

opened in 2007. owner / chef: thomas kolinikoff
$-$$: visa. mc
breakfast. lunch. treats. first come, first served

6th arr > **e10**

A friend who cooked for years at a bed and breakfast, told me: "You want breakfast just put an egg on it." Meaning almost anything can be served at breakfast *avec an oeuf. Coco & Co* seems to have expanded on this idea. Everything at this tiny café comes with an egg, but not just in a breakfast type of way. The cocotte burger is a deliciously seasoned, fresh-cut patty served with a sunny side egg on top. The richness infused by the yolk makes the burger like a tartare and is ultra satisfying. Don't worry about the cholesterol—there is always *le Lipitor*.

imbibe / devour:
orange presse
pastis
cocotte burger
brunch special
financier du jour
oeufs de saumon
tartinettes de villette canal
oeufs mayo

cococook

delicious food to go

3 rue charlot. between rue pastourelle and rue de bretagne
metro 8: filles du calvaire
33 (0) 1 42 74 80 00 www.cococook.com
mon - sun 11:30a - 9:30p

opened in 2009. chef: christophe reissfelder
$-$$: visa. mc
lunch. dinner. first come, first served

3rd arr > **e11**

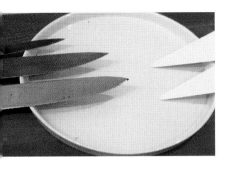

Sure, eating out in Paris is fantastic, but there are rules and confines. Eight pm is the earliest seating, and if you don't have a reservation, it's panic time. Thankfully, eating *in* in Paris can be pretty great also, especially when it involves good food, good wine and good friends. But you need to know where to get the take-out. No need to have panic time—*Cococook* is an excellent option. It's like visiting your chef friend's refrigerator; the foods here are healthy and scrumptious. And those who prefer sleep over nightlife can have friends over to eat and still be in bed by 11. Perfect.

imbibe / devour:
06 les grimaudes
jus rouge
salade carottes aux herbes
sandwich cococlub
soupe de petits pois & amandes
milanaise aux légumes & pesto
poulet fermier au quinoa
cake chocolat & courgette

cul de poule

another fun bistro
53 rue des martyrs. corner of rue victor massé. metro 2: pigalle
33 (0) 1 53 16 13 07
mon - sat noon - 2:30p, 8 - 11p

opened in 2008. owners: remi crespo and yannig samot chef: danielle semprun
$-$$: visa. mc
lunch. dinner. reservations recommended

18th arr > **e12**

Even though I'm a total francophile, sometimes French humor leaves me scratching my head. Jerry Lewis? Don't get it. But the comedy *Delicatessen*—about a butcher selling human meat—now that's entertainment! Along those lines (not the human meat ones, mind you) is *Cul de Poule*. Translation: Chicken Butt. This bistro is the talk of Paris, and it's as much about fun as it is about great food. Though handling ingredients sourced from top farmers and producers is no laughing matter, and the food here is no joke, I've noticed everything tastes better when it's served with a wink and a smile.

imbibe / devour:
08 domaine catherine et pierre breton bourgueil
06 gerard schueller pinot blanc
basque charcuterie
bavarois de petits pois
dorade rôtie sur peau et courgette
agneau épicé with aubergine confit
fromage du moment
crème mousseuse de chocolat au lait

31

du pain et des idées

stellar bread and pastries in a stunning space
34 rue yves toudic. corner rue de marseille. metro 5: jacques bonsargent
33 (0) 1 42 40 44 52 www.dupainetdesidees.com
mon - fri 6:45a - 8p

opened in 2002. owner / chef: christophe vasseur
$: visa. mc
treats. first come, first served

10th arr >

Was it Mr. Atkins who made eating bread a guilt-ridden event? If so I want to punch him in the face. Or better yet, I would like to take him with me to the gorgeous *du Pain et des Idées* and make him sit, surrounded by the tremendous pastries. Then I would consume a chunk of the signature *pain des amis* inches from him, with its chewy texture balanced by a hearth-darkened crust. I'd eat it simply with salted butter, and never offer a crumb. Then I'd cut off another slice for myself and toss him a protein bar. Take that, Atkins.

imbibe / devour:
pain des amis
escargot chocolat-pistache
mouna
tarte aux pommes
mini pavés
tarte aux peche
pain aux raisin
tarte citron

33

ets lion

general store

7 rue des abbesses. corner of rue houdon. metro 12: abbesses
33 (0) 46 06 64 71 www.epicerie-lion.fr
tue - sat 10:30a - 8p sun 11a - 7p

opened in 1997. owner: sophie ronti
$-$$: all major credit cards accepted
grocery. treats. first come, first served

18th arr >

A visit to the ultra-touristic Sacre Coeur is a must for any visitor to Paris—but don't let the performance of the mega-talented silver robot man miming to French pop music get in the way of the sweeping views. When you're done with the show, take a stroll to Rue des Abbesses. Surprisingly the tourists will stay behind (for the next robot performance?) and you will find yourself in a charming neighborhood. Here lives *Ets Lion*, circa 1895, the de facto general store of the area. Browse the garden section and the fine foods and sample some candies knowing you are safe from robot man.

imbibe / devour:
carombes réglisse
le calisson
fruits confits
le monarque gateau
le petit nice thè
sirops de fruits confits
bougie candles
bulk huile d'olive

glou

a food insiders take on cozy dining

101 rue vieille du temple. between rue des quatre fils and rue du perche
metro 8: saint-sébastien froissart
33 (0) 1 42 74 44 32 www.glou-resto.com
mon - sun noon - 2:30, 8 - 11p

opened in 2009. owners: julien fouin and ludovic dardenay
$$: all major credit cards accepted
lunch. dinner. reservations recommended

3rd arr >

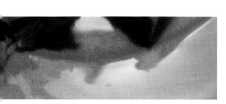

With the closing of many of America's beloved magazines comes lots of unemployed, creative people with time on their hands. I say that when a setback comes, it's an opportunity to do something you've always wanted. Julien is an example of this. After his stint as the editor of France's premier food magazine *Régal* ended, he opened *Glou*. This warm and inviting bistro has a super wine selection and specializes in simple fare made exceptionally well. I say *Glou* is the culmination of years of writing about food. Ruth Reichl are you listening?

imbibe / devour:
07 pierre gaillard rhône
06 meursault bouchères premier cru
lardo di colonnata de fausto guadagni
palette ibérico bellota
le tartare, 100% viande d'aubrac
echine de cochon basque
roquefort vieux berger
la fondante tarte au chocolat et à l'orange

higuma

restorative japanese fare
32 bis rue saint anne. corner of rue villego
163 rue saint-honoré. corner avenue de l'opera
metro 1: palais royal - musée du louvre
mon - sun 11:30a - 10:30p

opened in 1990
$-$$: visa. mc
lunch. dinner. first come, first served

1st arr > e16

Yes, I love French food. Rich, meaty *plats* are divine —but too much offal can really throw your system for a loop. The antidote to this is bright, clean flavors and satisfying, nurturing dishes. In Paris, I get this respite at *Higuma*. One plate of gyoza can counter all of those livers and gizzards and get me back to neutral, fast. I think of this place as a reset button transporting me back to my factory default settings. Obviously I'm not the only one who feels this way, as *Higuma* has a new second location. Keep this address in your back pocket, and you won't need that roll of Tums.

imbibe / devour:
heineken
jasmine tea
shoyu ramen
miso ramen
killer gyoza
yakinikudon
kimchi ramen
butter corn ramen

jean nicot

in search of a delicious croque monsieur
173 rue saint-honoré. between rue des pyramides and rue de l'echelle
metro 1: palais royal - musée du louvre
33 (0) 1 42 60 49 77
mon - fri 7:30a - 9 sat - sun 9a - 8p

opened in 1910
$: visa. mc
lunch. dinner. coffee / tea. snacks. first come, first served

1st arr > **e17**

I have searched high and low in this backwater food town for a brasserie that creates a gastronomically superior, fabulously gooey, croque monsieur. Sadly the best croque I have ever eaten was in Seattle. For shame, Paris. This is like saying the best grilled cheese you ever ate was in Tibet. But then I visited a particularly photogenic tabac called *Jean Nicot*. Finally—a hot, melty triad of meat, bread and cheese that measured up to my fantasies of what a real croque monsieur should be! No need to gild the lily here, except for maybe a little mustard on the side.

imbibe / devour:
pelforth blonde
ricard
cafe créme
niçoise au thon
croque monsieur
croque saint-honoré
tartine savoyarde
assiette du fromage

la bague de kenza

maghreb (north african) pastries

106 rue saint-maur. between rue oberkampf and rue jean-pierre timbaud
metro 3: parmentier
33 (0) 1 43 14 93 15
mon - sat 9a - 6p

opened in 1991. owners: l'hassen rahmani and samira fahim
$: cash only
treats. first come, first served

11th arr >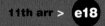

The first time I ever tried sushi, I was more motivated by the way that it looked than dying to taste raw fish. In other words I was attracted to the packaging and discovered I loved the contents. Sampling the Algerian pastries at *La Bague de Kenza* was similar. The mini watermelon-shaped pastries were gorgeous, so I was intent on eating one. All the pastries here are Maghreb and are filled with honey and nuts, and the essences of orange and rose waters. Everywhere you look, there are neatly arranged piles. Close your eyes, point a finger and whatever comes your way will be both pretty to look at and good to eat.

imbibe / devour:
tea
rfisse
baklava
cravatte pistache
dziriate
mhajeb
kesra
ghribia

la cabane à huîtres

incredible oysters

4 rue antoine bourdelle. between avenue du maine and rue falguière
metro 4 / 6 / 12 / 13: montparnasse
33 (0) 1 45 49 47 27
wed - sat 12:30 - 3p, 7 - 11p

owner / chef: francis dubourg
$: cash only
lunch. dinner. reservations recommended

15th arr > e19

Here's the secret behind *La Cabane à Huîtres*. It's located a block from Gare Montparnasse, which serves France's Atlantic coast, and Francis has oyster beds near Bordeaux on that coast. So the oysters at *La Cabane,* which is no bigger than an American SUV, are ridiculously fresh. The 22 people that can wedge in here slurp the briny bivalves as fast as the cheerful Francis can shuck them, with everybody helping to pass *plateaus* across the room because it's too crowded for personal delivery. I helped myself to another glass of wine and marveled at what might be the perfect restaurant.

imbibe / devour:
07 entre deux mers
08 loupiac cérons
huîtres moyennes
huîtres grosses
tranche foie gras
magret de canard fumé
fromage pyrénées
canelé

la cantine de quentin

top-notch food for a bargain

52 rue bichat. between quai de jemmapes and rue de la grange aux belles
metro 4: gare de l'est
33 (0) 1 42 02 40 32
lunch tue - sun noon - 3:30p store 10a - 7:30p

opened in 2007. owner: jacques mailnot
chefs: johann baron and quentin hoffman
$-$$: visa. mc
lunch. grocery. reservations recommended

10th arr > **e20**

Most people speak of our pallid economy as a negative. Always the optimist, I can think of an upside. As a response to the economic downturn, young, clever chefs are opening small neighborhood bistros with a focus on high-quality food but with economical prices. This is clearly illustrated at *La Cantine de Quentin*. Here you get top-shelf caliber, but the price tag of buck-night at your local sports bar. Daily lunch menus of hearty, deftly prepared dishes are served in a charming wine shop meets epicerie environment. And no drunk guys yelling at big-screen TVs. Score!

imbibe / devour:
badoit
07 domaine les grands bois côtes du rhône
terrine de campagne maison
velouté d'artichauts
ravioles de royans
tartare de boeuf au couteau
poulet fermier rôti
cheesecake de johann

la cave à bulles

french artisanal beer store
45 rue quincampoix. between rue berger and rue rambuteau
metro 11: rambuteau
33 (0) 1 40 29 03 69 www.caveabulles.fr
tue - sat 10a - 2p, 4 - 8p

opened in 2006. owner: simon thillou
$-$$: visa. mc
first come, first served

4th arr >

In wine-loving France, beer is like the earthworm of the alcohol world. It is underappreciated, undervalued and hard to find. That is until *La Cave à Bulles* opened. Simon, who is quite charismatic and not worm-like at all, is spreading the word about beers of this country. I am not kidding when I divulge, though I have been traveling to Paris for well over a decade, I have neither heard nor tasted 90% of the beers available here. Simon realizes there's lots of work to do, which is why he offers classes to small groups to educate about *les beers*. Here's mud in your eye!

imbibe / devour:
beers:
  thomas becket bière de bourgogne
  northem blanche
  juliette-brasserie uberach
  la chardon rouge
  la bière des collines
  ninkasi triple
  la clandestine

la crémerie

natural wine shop and small plates
9 rue des quatre vents. between rue de condé and rue de seine. metro 4: odéon
33 (0) 1 43 54 99 30 www.lacremerie.fr
lunch fri - sat 1 - 2:30p dinner tue - sat 5:30 - 10p wine shop opens at 10:30a

opened in 2001. owners: serge et hélène mathieu
$$: visa. mc
lunch. dinner. reservations recommended

6th arr > **e22**

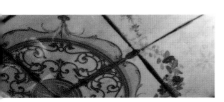

Follow me here. Natural wines are different than organic wines in that they are produced without the aid of any commercial processes. Instead, they are harvested by hand and fermented with wild yeasts. This process produces interesting, esoteric wines usually from tiny producers. My wine-freak friends seek out these natural vinos like vampires on *Trueblood* tired of the synthetic stuff. Me? I just go to *La Crémerie*. Not only is their selection unsurpassed, the room is (surprise!) housed in a former *crémerie* which is perfectly charming.

imbibe / devour:
06 arbois pupillin, le ginglet
07 philippe pacalet ruchottes-chambertin
champagne billecart-salmon
eau de vie de poire william
plateau de iberiques
paté de canard
boudin noir sur pan grillé
conserverie st. christophe terrine artisanale

la pâtisserie des rêves

dream pastries

93 rue du bac. corner of rue de varenne. metro 12: rue du bac
33 (0)1 42 84 00 82 www.lapatisseriedesreves.com
tue - sat 10a - 8:30p sun 8a - 2p

opened in 2009. owner / chef: philippe conticini
$-$$: visa. mc
treats. first come, first served

6th arr >

La Pâtisserie des Rêves, the pastry shop of your dreams, is as advertised—the experience of buying something here is as fantastical as the treat itself. Famed pastry guru Philippe has staged the space like a Roald Dahl book. Buttery delicacies are displayed like rare and prized specimens under a network of glass cloches. To get a closer look, you simply ask for a cloche to be lifted, setting in motion pulleys and counterweights, all part of the elaborate Oompa Loompa type set-up. This might feel gimmicky if the confections weren't so exquisite. But don't worry Charlie, you need no golden ticket to enter.

imbibe / devour:
le grand cru
le mille-feuille du dimanche
le moka
le st. honoré
le paris-brest
les éclaires
le tarte tatin
les viennoiseries

la pharmacie

a cheerful neighborhood bistro

22 rue jean-pierre timbaud. corner rue du grand prieuré. metro 3: oberkampf
33 (0) 1 55 28 75 98 www.lapharmacie.net
mon - sun noon - 2:30p, 8p - midnight

opened in 2009. owner: max brasserd chef: christophe bearraux
$$: visa. mc
lunch. dinner. reservations recommended

11th arr >

With a name like *La Pharmacie* you'd expect to feel good after eating at this charming restaurant housed in an old pharmacy. But what I discovered while eating here, is that it wasn't just the delicious food that perked me up. *La Pharmacie* is like a happy pill and the whole neighborhood is taking the prescription. A birthday party was happening in one corner with friends lifting their glasses to the birthday boy. A couple sitting next to me struck up a conversation, giving me their hottest tips on the Paris restaurant scene. I left here totally sated. No need for Zoloft after.

imbibe / devour:
08 cuvée des galets
07 gimonnet-gonet brut
terrine à la moment
le burger normandaise avec foie gras
faison rôti avec celeri & marrons
gnocchi & escargot
pied de cochon avec tartelette
caramel à la fleur de sel "damnation"

le balzar

traditional brasserie
49 rue des ecoles. between boulevard saint-michel and rue de la sorbonne
metro 10: cluny la sorbonne
33 (0) 1 43 54 13 67 www.brasseriebalzar.com
mon - sun 8p - midnight

opened in 1898. owners: the flo people
$$: all major credit cards accepted
dinner. full bar. reservations recommended

5th arr > **e25**

Here's a Parisian dining primer. Restaurants are generally formal, bistros are moderately priced neighborhood places with simple food. Brasseries offer even simpler fare like the "classics"—steak frites or roast chicken—and usually have an outside terrace which can lead to some boisterous streetside dining. There are many quintessential Paris brasseries, each attracting a distinct clientele from streetwalkers to society types. *Le Balzar* is my favorite. Because it attracts an always-entertaining fashion-crowd, *Balzar* satisfies my eyes as much as my stomach.

imbibe / devour:
kir royale
pommery royal brut
poireaux vinaigrette
foie de veau poêlé
poulet rôti
steak frites
gigot d'agneau fermier du quercy
baba au rhum

le baratin

incredible food influenced by france, italy and argentina
3 rue jouye rouve. between rue de belleville and rue lesage. metro 11: pyrénées
33 (0) 1 43 49 39 70
tue - fri noon - 2:30p 8 - 11p sat 8p - 11p

opened in 2006. owner: phillippe pinoteau chef: raquel carena
$$: visa. mc
lunch. dinner. reservations recommended

20th arr > **e26**

Once in awhile I taste food so good, I realize I am in the presence of someone with "the touch." Raquel, the chef at *Le Baratin* has "it." When I took a bite of the *colinot frit*, I instantly got "the feeling" and across my face was plastered "the look." To have "the touch" is a special talent where a chef makes food that tastes like no one else's—everything is just a little more: flavorful, delicate, nuanced. I don't think you can learn "the touch;" you must be born with it. I don't have "it," that's to be sure—so I'll just eat the food of those that do have "it" and be supremely happy.

imbibe / devour:
07 bourgogne hautes côtes de beaune
muscat de patras
tarte de blettes & parmesan
boullon de cabillaud et tomates
colinot frit, sauce grinich
collier d'agneau aux epices, riz basmati
fromage blanc
crème de noisette

le chateaubriand

sexy, creative cuisine
129 avenue parmentier
between rue du faubourg du temple and rue de la fountaine au roi
metro 11: goncourt
33 (0) 1 43 57 45 95 tue - sat 8p - midnight

opened in 2007. owner / chef: inaki aizpitarte   owner: frédéric peneau
$$-$$$: visa. mc
dinner. reservations recommended

11th arr > **e27**

Recent articles have mentioned support groups developing for people depressed that they can't live in the iridescent fantasy world depicted in *Avatar*. Really? Get a fishtank! If you want to experience something truly sad, go to Le Chateaubriand and realize you won't be able to eat there every night. This fantasy world has chantilly colored walls washed in golden light—a perfect backdrop for the pack of fetching waiters who deliver the inventive food which is as surprising as it is comforting. *Le Chateaubriand* is spectacular. No 3D glasses required.

imbibe / devour:
07 rené mosse anjou rouge
pommery champagne
encorrnets, carottes, bouguignonne
st pierre, cresson, liseron d'eau, cowbawa
veau d'hugo, radis, navets, foie de morue
poire crumble, mahaleb
chocolat, framboises
fromages du jour

le janissaire

turkish cuisine with the trip

22 - 24 allée vivaldi. between rue de reuilly and rue hénard. metro 8: daumesnil
33 (0) 1 43 40 37 37 www.lejanissaire.fr
lunch mon - fri noon - 2:30p dinner mon - sat 7 - 11:30p

opened in 2001. owner: karaman mustafa
$$: visa. mc
lunch. dinner. reservations accepted

12th arr >

Most people who look forward to *manging* in Paris think primarily about the unpasteurized cheeses, delicacies in shells and buttery sauces. But this is nearsighted as this is one of the most culturally diverse cities anywhere. A main destination of Turks and North Africans emmigrating to Europe means killer kabobs and couscous are easily found. *Le Janissaire* is a fine example of where to get yummy meaty bites on a stick. Located in the somewhat far-flung 12th arr., you'd best think ahead before visiting here. But the tender grilled chunks of lamb are worth the trip—they're a turkish delight.

imbibe / devour:
buzbag turkish red wine
domaine jacky touraine gamay
beignet de calamar
foie d'agneau poêle aux oignons assaisonne
cuisse de poulet au fromage & coulis de tomate
onglet de boeuf grillé au gros sel
nois de saint jacques tava
patlican tatli - aubergines confites

les papilles

food worthy of a michelin star and wine store
30 rue gay lussac. corner of rue saint-jacques. rer b: luxembourg
33 (0) 1 43 25 20 79 www.lespapillesparis.com
mon - sat noon - 2p, 7:30 - 10p

opened in 2003. owner: bertrand bluy chef: ulric claude
$$: visa. mc
lunch. dinner. reservations recommended

5th arr >

Remember in movies when the food would arrive under a gigantic silver cover? The unveiling of the dish always impressed me as elegance with a capital E. It's sad that these food domes seem to have fallen out of favor. At the stylishly homey bistro and wine cave, *Les Papilles*, the food is served in the country equivalent—gorgeous tin-lined french copper pots. When my own personal copper pot arrived, the waiter removed the lid. As the gush of steam evaporated (my face felt dewy and renewed), it revealed a cauldron filled with bubbling, herb-infused meat and wine. I felt like I was a somebody.

imbibe / devour:
08 domaine vacheron sancerre
eau de vie
lomo de thon
foie gras de canard à l'ancienne
le boudin blanc béarnais
assiette de jambon mr. arosagaray
les fraises des bois
felée d'agrumes au campari

le train bleu

like dining in le louvre
1er étage gare de lyon. place louis armand. metro 1: gare de lyon
33 (0) 1 43 43 09 06 www.le-train-bleu.com
mon - sat 11:30a - 3p, 7 - 11p (bar open all day)

opened in 1901. chef: jean-pierre hocquet
$$-$$$: all major credit cards accepted
lunch. dinner. snacks. full bar. first come, first served

12th arr > **e30**

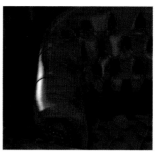

2009 was an epic travel year for me. In a two-month span I was in six major cities in four countries. (Thank you *eat.shop* guides!) Seeing that many cities, one after another, illuminated their differences, with Paris being all about splendor and magnificence. An awe-inspiring example of this is *Le Train Bleu*, the belle époque restaurant in the Gare de Lyon. It is resplendent (so excited to finally be able to use this word). I rarely eat here as it's quite spendy—but for a cup of tea, or a bottle of wine and some nibbles it's a worthwhile expenditure as this is a place of special beauty.

imbibe / devour:
"la lune bleue" ceylon tea
06 alsace dopff & irion gewurztraminer
isle flotant
brioche pain perdue avec glace
poitrine de veau oubliée
escargot bourgogne
crémeuse de bisque de homard
baba au rhum

67

le verre volé

natural wine shop and small plates
67 rue de lancry. corner of quai de valmy. metro 5: jacques bonsergent
www.leverrevole.fr 33 (0) 1 48 03 17 34
mon - sun noon - 2:30p, 7:30 - 11p

opened in 2000. owner: cyril bordarier
$-$$: visa. mc
lunch. dinner. reservations recommended

10th arr > e31

Wine sometimes costs less than a bottle of Perrier in France, so it's easy to make the leap that this might be a country of winos. It's the exact opposite. Really good wines at good prices seems to educate and cultivate the general public who seem more interested in quality than quantity. Which in turn supports places like *Le Verre Volé*. At this tiny cave, bottles from small, interesting producers line the walls. One can buy and fly, or order a bottle with a plate of the hearty fare for seven euros over the bottle price. This is great way to try compelling vintages—and a far cry from the Three Buck Chuck experience.

imbibe / devour:
07 oliver cousa
06 morgon gamay noir
06 anjou aoc
la salade d'endive jambon cru
le boudin noir confiture d'oignons
le terrine de campagne
tartare de saumon "graveaux"
petite suisse de malo

l'ourcine

chef driven bistro

92 rue broca. between boulevard arago and boulevard de port-royal
metro 6: denfert rochereau
33 (0) 1 47 07 13 65
tue - sat noon - 2:30p, 7 - 10:30p

opened in 2004. owner / chef: sylvain danière
$$: visa. mc
lunch. dinner. reservations recommended

13th arr > **e32**

Paris' magnificent buildings and rich cultural history make it the most touristed city on earth. Think of it as Euro Disney for grown-ups. Since it is a tourist mecca—there are numerous traps, especially when it comes to dining—real gems can be hard to find. *L'Ourcine* is located on a street you would never just happen down, yet you should definitely find. Opened by celebrated chef Sylvain Danière, his take on the classics are marvelous. The fact that dining in this warm, homey environment is also affordable, means there really are real treasures in this magic kingdom.

imbibe / devour:

consommé de sauvageon juste crème,
   croutons & ciboulette
filet mignon de porc rôti à l'ail confit
dos de sanglier cuisiné au beurre persillé
pigeon rôti au foie gras de canard
fricassée minute de champignons des bois
feuilletée de pommes flambées au calvados,
   caramel glace

71

mamie gâteaux

salon de thé
66 rue du cherche-midi. corner of rue de l'abbé grégoire
metro 4: saint-placide
33 (0) 1 42 22 32 15 www.mamie-gateaux.com
tue - sat 11:30a - 6p

opened in 2003. owner: hervé duplessis owner / chef: mariko duplessis
$-$$: cash only
lunch. coffee / tea. treats. first come, first served

6th arr > **e33**

I used to think "ladies who lunch" had a rather glamorous occupation. I practically based my entire career on the idea of it. But seeing one too many St. John clad ladies air kissing and sipping on a lipstick marked glass of chardonnay made me recoil. My fantasy and reality were way off. What I had in mind was more in the vein of *Mamie Gâteaux*. This tea salon exudes quiet chic. Delicate quiches and savory cakes served with a light salad are the perfect nosh for a social lunch. So wear something truly stylish here and leave the St. John at home.

imbibe / devour:
thé mariage frères-bourbon
citron-miel
tarte tomates, aubergines, jambon cru
cake saumon fenouil
cake pruneaux lardons
crumble de legumes
salade with saumon fumé, tomates confites
tarte aux figues

marché avenue du président wilson

shopping for food as only the french can

avenue du président wilson. between rue debrousse and place d'iéna
metro 9: alma marceau or iéna
wed and sat 7:30a - approximately 2:30p

$ - $$: cash only
market. first come, first served

I don't care for the "trip of a lifetime" mentality where you have to visit all of the "must-see" spots on a claustrophobic tour bus. Yuck. The marvel of Paris comes from walking its streets. Crossing over the Pont Royal and realizing you are going through the massive, ornate gates of the Louvre is astounding every time. Similarly, shopping at one of the Parisian street food markets can provide drool-inducing memories. One of the toniest markets is on Avenue Président Wilson. Abundance is the theme here. I guarantee you'll enjoy this more than seeing dead old Napoleon in his tomb.

imbibe / devour:
coquille saint jacques
escargot
saint-nectaire fromage
moulé à la main demi-sel croquant butter
cêpes
paté de campagne
crêpes from crêperie breton
fresh chevre

75

marie-anne cantin

a great cheese shop
12 rue du champ de mars. between avenue bosquet and rue duvivier
metro 8: école militaire
33 (0) 1 45 50 43 94 www.cantin.fr
mon 2 - 7:30p tue - sat 8:30a - 7:30p sun 8:30a - 1p

opened in 1982. owners: marie-anne and antoine cantin
$-$$: visa. mc
grocery. first come, first served

7th arr >

I may never know the answer to this nagging question: Does food taste better in its native environment, or does the excitement about being in the place heighten one's senses? For example, if I were to magically transport one of *Marie-Anne Cantin's* fabulous Roqueforts to my home in Portland, would it taste as phenomenal as when consumed in the shadow of the Eiffel Tower? Though Marie's stock of award-winning cheeses are among the best in Paris, would I feel the same about them stateside? Since my friends at U.S. Customs won't let me answer this question, it will remain a great mystery.

imbibe / devour:
fromage:
  saint marcellin sensation
  bacaffe sèche
  mucols
  bleu de saqueville
  tomme de savoie
  fontainebleu maison
  beurre cru, m.a. cantin

CANTIN
Beurre cru à la Baratte
Demi-sel

mi-va-mi

some of the best falafels in paris
23 rue des rosiers. near rue des ecouffes. metro 1: saint paul
33 (0) 42 71 53 72
mon - thu 11a - midnight fri 11a - 7p sun 11a - midnight

opened in 1998
$: visa. mc
lunch. dinner. wine / beer. first come, first served

4th arr > e36

Where I live, there's something called "The Oregon Vortex." Though bumper stickers are offered up as proof, I'm a skeptic. I can, however, prove there is a Paris vortex. A corner in the Marais is home to not one, but two of the best falafel shops in the world: *L' As du Falafel* (featured in the first edition) and *Mi-Va-Mi* directly across the street. It's totally different in style from its competitor but just as good (maybe better). The only thing to do is try them both and decide for yourself. And don't forget to buy your "Paris Vortex" bumper sticker, checks payable to: Jon's Awesome Business.

imbibe / devour:
jus naturel
heineken
pita falafel
pita chawarma
brochette dinde
assiette keftas
assiette de frites
pita merguez

passage 53

gloriously nuanced cuisine

53 passage des panoramas. between boulevard poissonnière and rue saint-marc
metro 8 / 9: grand boulevards
33 (0) 1 42 33 04 35 www.passage53.com
mon - sat 12:30 - 2:30p, 8p - close

opened in 2009. owner: hugo desnoyer chef: m. sato
$$$: visa. mc
lunch. dinner. reservations recommended

2nd arr > **e37**

Even though I eat for a living, the number of lunches I've spent over $100 on is small. At dinner I'll open the wallet, but my Midwest upbringing makes it hard for me to give it up at lunch. At *Passage 53*, I had a change of heart. This beautifully spare place located in the beautifully ornate Passage Panoramas is a celebration of subtlety. With nuance and virtuosity, Sato sent out the courses (either five or eight). Prepared like minimalist assemblages, their delicate perfection commands you to delight in their flawless balance. One bite and I realized I was eating small masterpieces. I would have paid any price.

imbibe / devour:
jacquesson champagne
degustation menu:
  pumpkin with coffee foam
  veal tartare with raw oyster
  calamari on almond & cauliflower cream
  olive oil poached salmon with radishes
  pork loin with baby root vegetables
  banana mont blanc

pink flamingo pizza

pizza with attitude

105 rue vieille du temple. corner of rue des quatre fils. metro 8: filles du calvaire
67 rue bichat. corner of rue de la grange aux belles. metro 5: jacques bonsergent
33 (0) 1 42 02 31 70 www.pinkflamingopizza.com
mon 7 - 11:30p tue - sat noon - 3p, 7 - 11:30p sun 1 - 11p

opened in 2004. owner / chef: jamie young owner: marie ravel
$-$$: visa. mc
lunch. dinner. wine / beer. first come, first served

10th arr >

How is it that a long-necked bird, exotic and pink, in-spired everything from neon nightclub signs to large, gun-toting female impersonators? I will say that *Pink Flamingo Pizza* seems to have more in common with the latter as it caters to a largely young, bohemian set. Pods of friends hang out along the banks of the canal with helium balloons used to identify their or-der. With the sometimes witty names and unusual combinations of ingredients, *Pink Flamingo* has a sort of puckish attitude that is as appealing as the pies. I'd say, the bird is the word!

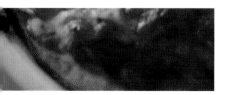

imbibe / devour:
pelforth
pizzas:
  la bjork (smoked salmon, egg & créme fraîche)
  l'aphrodite (eggplant, hummus & pimento)
  l'almodovar (paella on pizza)
  la che (cubano pizza)
cheesecake

pozzetto

silky gelato majesty

39 rue du roi de sicile. between rue vieille du temple and rue du bourg-tibourg
metro 1: saint paul
33 (0) 1 42 77 08 64 www.pozzetto.biz
mon - thu 10a - 10:30p fri - sat 10a - midnight sun 10a - 11p

opened in 2008. owners: daniele and paolo maua
$: mc. visa
treats. coffee / tea

4th arr > e39

Normally, I quiver with excitement to eat *Pozzetto's* gelato. It's the perfect respite after a long day of shopping in the Marais. However on the day I was last there, in the middle of November, the temperature was near freezing and a concoction of frozen eggs and cream wasn't too appealing. Still, I was on the clock, so I ordered from the bored employee. I took a few pictures then sat on a nearby bench and continued to do my job—eating the gelato. As it started to sleet, a man approached and said, "Where do I find such a magnificent treat?" I pointed to *Pozzetto* and happily got back to work.

imbibe / devour:
gelato:
  gianduja torinese
  pistacchio di sicilia
  nocciola piemonte
  fior di latte
  cioccolato fondente
  yogurt magro
  stracciatella

racines

simple and stellar food, natural wines

8 passage des panoramas. between boulevard poissonnière and rue saint-marc
metro 8 / 9: grand boulevards
33 (0) 1 40 13 06 41 www.morethanorganic.com
mon - fri 12:30 - 2:30p, 8p - midnight

opened in 2007. owner: david lanher chef: sven chartier
$$-$$$: visa. mc
lunch. dinner. wine. reservations recommended

2nd arr > e40

Upon tasting the braised pork and root vegetables at *Racines*, I was smitten. I find this to be one of the most satisfying food combos: robust proteins with a delectable side. It feels like masculine food, but prepared with a delicate touch. I finished the food and a bottle of gorgeous riesling and left with a serious man-crush. In subsequent days, I would try many other restaurants but never shake the memory of the perfectly seared scallops served under a silken blanket of lardo that I had adored here. Eating at other places felt like cheating on my true love. *Racines*, you had me at hello.

imbibe / devour:
06 emmanuel houillon arbois pupillin
07 gérard schueller riesling
07 comté de marcel petite
saint jacques de bretagne au lard
foie gras "extra" aux pommes
cochon de lait "noir de bigorre," rutabaga au lard
poularde "racine," petites légumes
dos de bar de ligne, poireaux à l'huile de sésame

supernature

super natural dining

12 rue de trévise. between rue de montyon and rue richer
metro 8 / 9: grand boulevards
33 (0) 1 47 70 21 03 www.super-nature.fr
mon - fri noon - 2:30p, 7 - 10:30p sat 7:30 - 11:30p sun 11:30a - 3:30p

opened in 2006. owner / chef: severine mourey
$-$$: visa. mc
lunch. dinner. brunch. reservations recommended

9th arr > **e41**

As I mentioned earlier in this book, healthy food in Paris is like the new bacon (veggie bacon perhaps?). Maybe this is too strong of a statement—but clean, healthy cuisine is certainly a breath of fresh air in this cheese-obsessed country. At *Supernature*, grains and sprouts are given their rightful recognition alongside lean proteins. In fact, coming to the popular Sunday brunch here is almost a throwback to the days of the old *Moosewood Cookbook*. I'm not complaining. I think healthy is the future. Even if this is simply a case of "what's old is new again," I've got my tie-dyed tank top ready to go.

imbibe / devour:
jus d'orange fraîchement pressé
risotto potimarron petits pois
tajine de poisson
cheeseburger aux jeunes pousses
oeuf cocotte bio au philadelphia cheese
carrot cake
ultra fondant au chocolate poivré
comté et figues

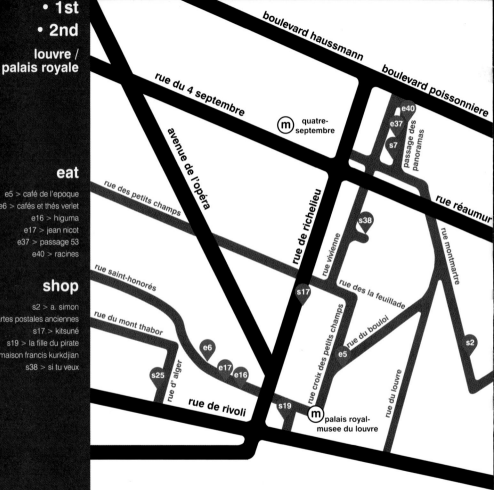

- **1st**
- **2nd**

**louvre /
palais royale**

eat

e5 > café de l'epoque
e6 > cafés et thés verlet
e16 > higuma
e17 > jean nicot
e37 > passage 53
e40 > racines

shop

s2 > a. simon
s7 > cartes postales anciennes
s17 > kitsuné
s19 > la fille du pirate
s25 > maison francis kurkdjian
s38 > si tu veux

boulevard haussmann

boulevard poissonniere

rue du 4 septembre

avenue de l'opéra

rue des petits champs

rue saint-honorés

rue du mont thabor

rue d' alger

rue de rivoli

ⓜ quatre-septembre

rue réaumur

rue de richelieu

rue vivienne

rue montmartre

rue des la feuillade

rue du bouloi

rue croix des petits champs

rue du louvre

passage des panoramas

ⓜ palais royal-musee du louvre

e40
e37
s7
s38
s17
e6
e17
e16
s25
s2
e5
s19

NORTH

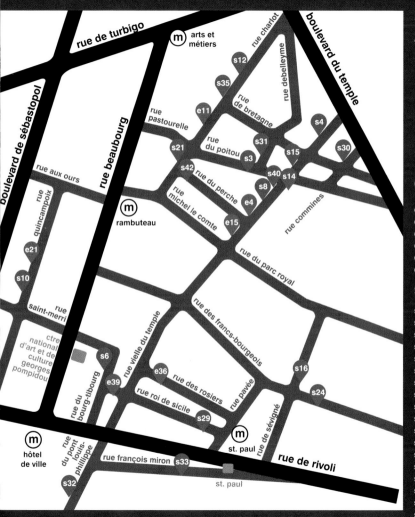

3rd •
4th •
le marais

eat

e4 > breizh café
e11 > cococook
e15 > glou
e21 > la cave à bulles
e36 > mi-va-mi
e39 > pozzetto

shop

s3 > avenches
s4 > balouga
s6 > calourette
s8 > chi.ind
s10 > comptoir des écritures
s12 > farida
s14 > french trotters
s15 > ie boutique
s16 > isaac reina
s21 > le bouclard
s24 > l'object
s29 > noir kennedy
s30 > norden
s31 > object sonore
s32 > papier +
s33 > petit pan
s35 > plagg
s40 > surface to air
s42 > tremblay alvergne

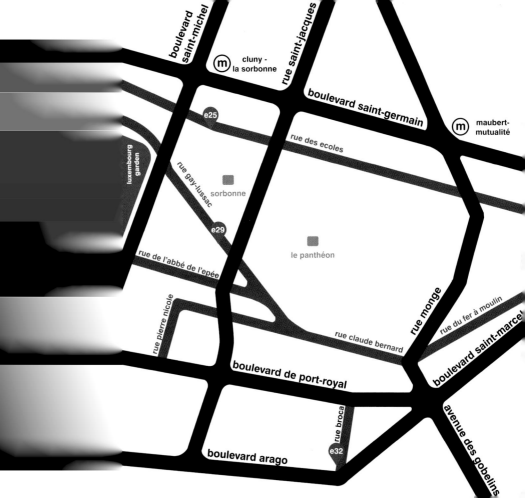

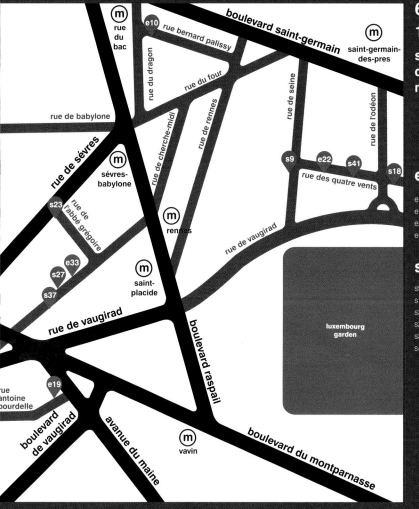

6th •
15th •

saint-germain-des-pres / montparnasse

eat

e10 > coco & co
e19 > la cabane à huîtres
e22 > la crémerie
e33 > mamie gateaux

shop

s9 > cire trudon
s18> kyrie eleison
s23 > les vélos parisiens
s27 > mamie gateaux brocante
s37 > serendipity
s41 > talc

eat

e7 > chapon chocolatier
e23 > la pâtisserie des rèves
e34 > marché avenue du président wilson
e35 > marie-anne cantin

shop

s11 > deyrolle

ave du prés. wilson
m alma-marceau
pont des invalides
quai d'orsay
pont de l'alma
quai branly
m invalides
eiffel tower
Champ de Mars
avenue bosquet
pont des invalides
esplanade des invalides
rue du champ de mars
rue de grenelle
e7
s11
avenue de tourville
rue de varenne
avenue de la motte-picquet
m la tour-maubourg
m varenne
e23
boulevard des invalides
rue du bac
boulevard garibaldi
rue de sévres
boulevard raspail
NORTH

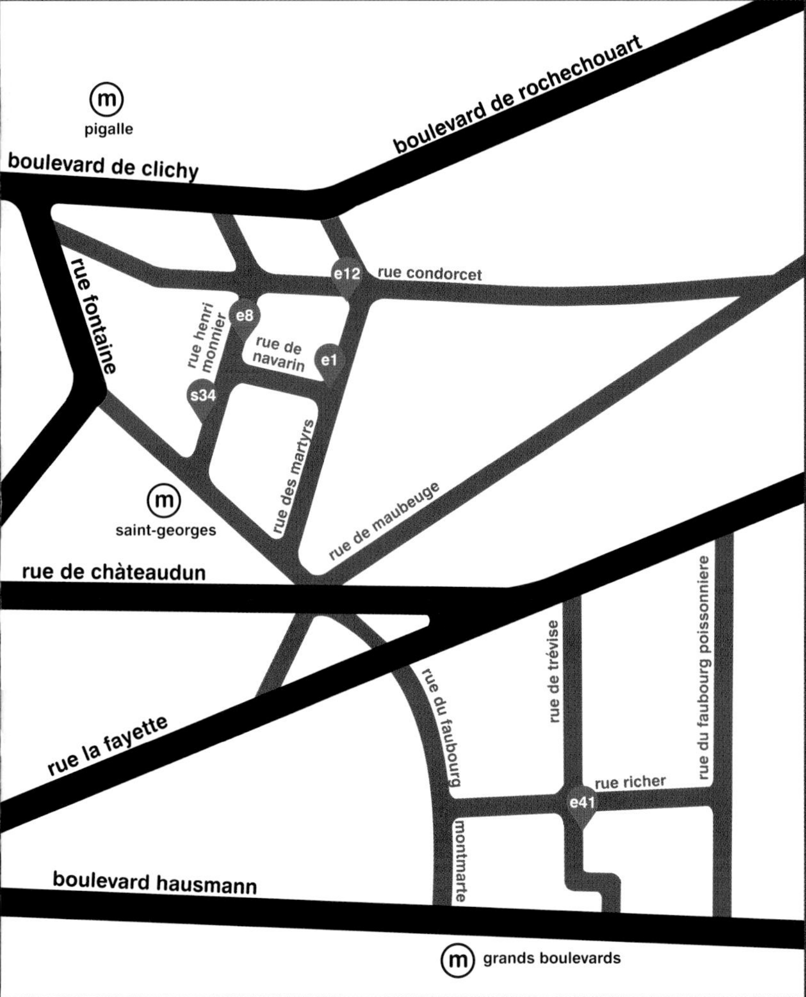

(m) pigalle

boulevard de rochechouart

boulevard de clichy

rue fontaine

e12 > rue condorcet

rue henri monnier

e8

rue de navarin

e1

s34

rue des martyrs

(m) saint-georges

rue de maubeuge

rue de chàteaudun

rue la fayette

rue du faubourg montmartre

rue de trévise

rue richer

e41

rue du faubourg poissonniere

boulevard hausmann

(m) grands boulevards

eat

e1 > arnaud delmontel
e8 > chauvoncourt
e12 > cul de poule
e41 > supernature

shop

s34 > pigalle

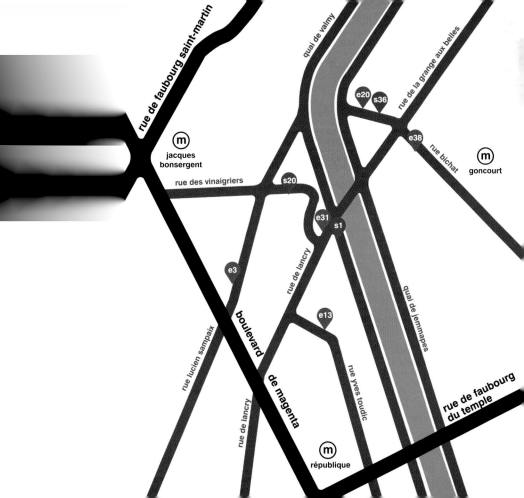

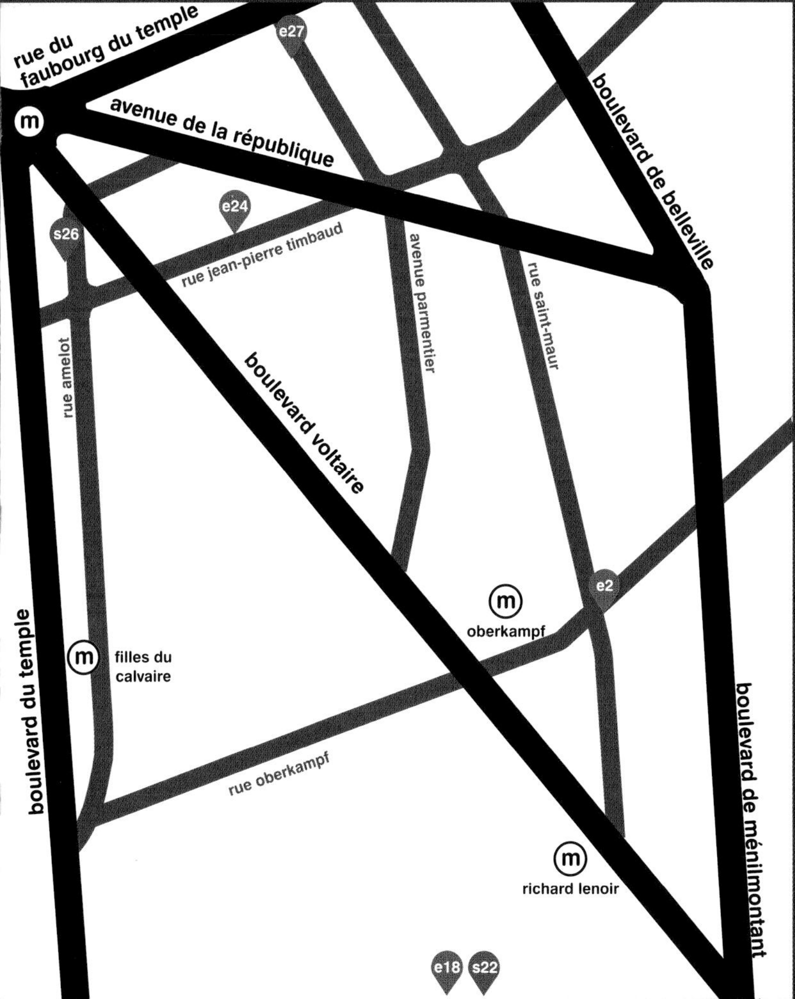

11th •
bastille

Map labels:

rue du faubourg du temple

avenue de la république

boulevard de belleville

boulevard voltaire

boulevard du temple

rue jean-pierre timbaud

rue amelot

avenue parmentier

rue saint-maur

rue oberkampf

boulevard de ménilmontant

e27

s26

e24

e2

(m) oberkampf

(m) filles du calvaire

(m) richard lenoir

e18 s22

eat

e2 > bistrot mélac
e18 > la bague de kenza
(off map)
e24 > la pharmacie
e27 > le chateaubriand

shop

s22 > le jeune fréres
(off map)
s26 > maison jean-baptiste

eat

e28 > le janissaire
e30 > le train bleu

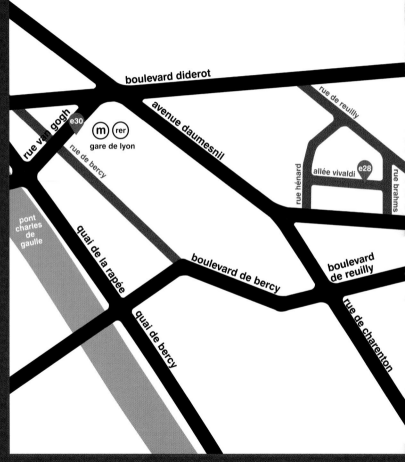

boulevard diderot

rue de reuilly

rue van gogh

avenue daumesnil

(m) (rer) e30
gare de lyon

rue de bercy

rue hénard

allée vivaldi e28

rue brahms

pont charles de gaulle

quai de la rapée

boulevard de bercy

boulevard de reuilly

quai de bercy

rue de charenton

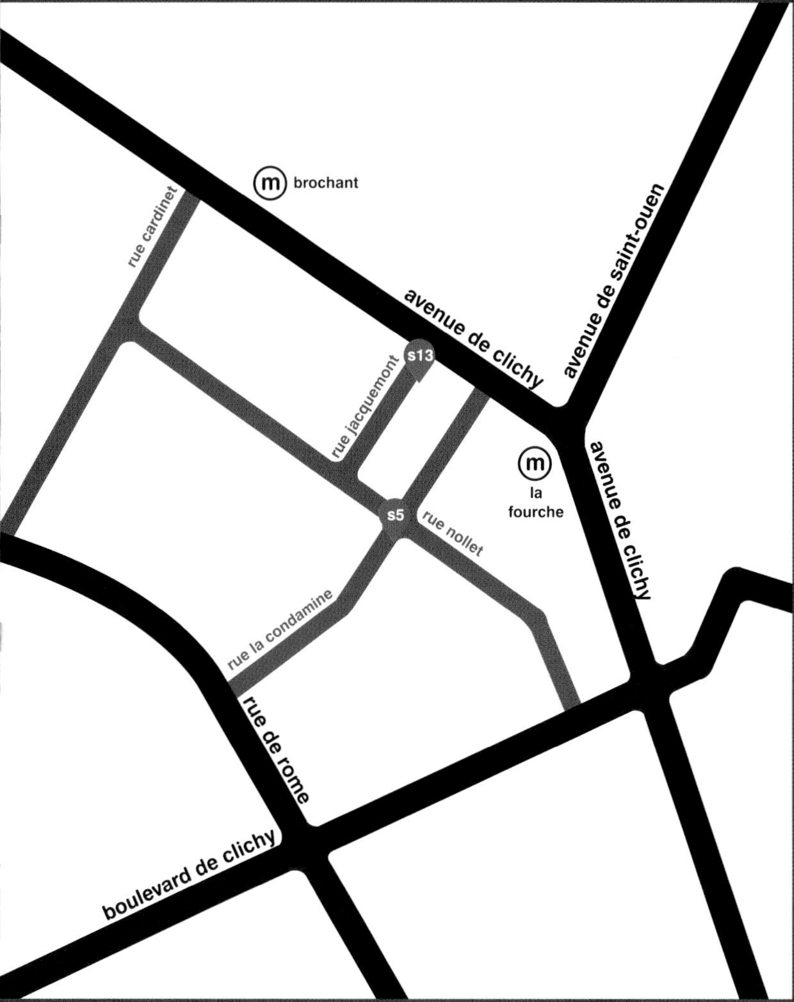

shop

s5 > bda
s13 > french touche

(m) brochant

rue cardinet

avenue de clichy

avenue de saint-ouen

s13

rue jacquemont

(m) la fourche

avenue de clichy

s5

rue nollet

rue la condamine

avenue de clichy

rue de rome

boulevard de clichy

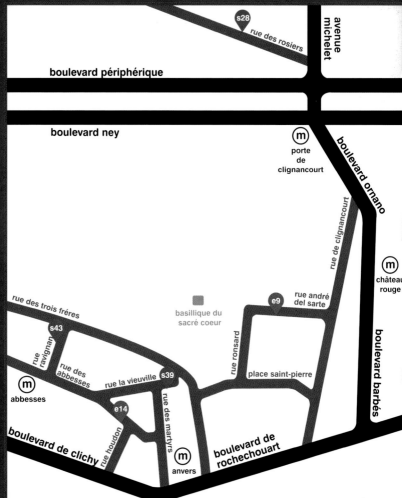

• 18th
montmarte

eat

e9 > chéri bibi
e14 > ets lion

shop

marché aux puces de
st. oeun
s39 > spree
s43 > zut!

s28
rue des rosiers

avenue
michelet

boulevard périphérique

boulevard ney

m
porte
de
clignancourt

boulevard ornano

rue de clignancourt

m
château
rouge

boulevard barbés

rue des trois fréres

s43

rue ravignan

rue des
abbesses

rue la vieuville

s39

m
abbesses

e14

rue houdon

rue des martyrs

basillique du
sacré coeur

rue ronsard

e9
rue andré
del sarte

place saint-pierre

m
anvers

boulevard de
rochechouart

boulevard de clichy

NORT

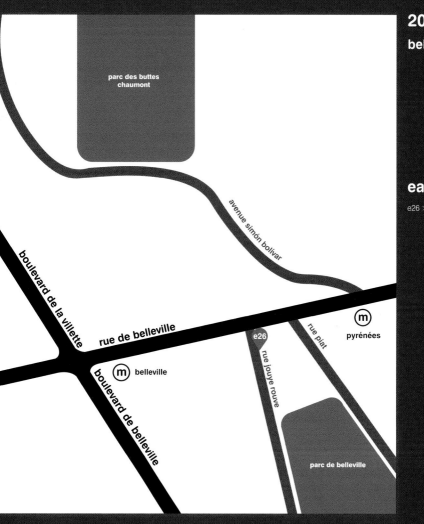

eat

e26 > le baratin

artazart

art and design bookstore

83 quai de valmy. corner rue de lancry. metro 5: jacques bonsergent
33 (0) 1 40 40 24 00 www.artazart.com
mon - fri 10:30a - 7:30p sat - sun 2 - 8p

opened in 1999. owner: carol huguenin
visa. mc
online shopping

10th arr > s01

People often ask which neighborhood in Paris I would choose to live in. Honestly, a dart thrown at a map would produce a satisfactory answer—as long as Charles de Gaulle airport were out of play. Okay, I might secretly aim for the Canal St. Martin. This 'hood has great restaurants, interesting shops and a community of young, creative types which makes it the middle of hipsterville. Also central, both geographically and in spirit, is *Artazart*—an art and design bookshop that opened when this area was still considered pioneering.

covet:
pinhole camera paint can
bensimon bags
lampe gras
"design & literature" by esther henwood
"swedish architecture in wood"
"paper, tear, fold, rip, crease, cut" by raven smith
credit card stickers
lampe gras 206 chromée

a. simon

hotel and restaurant supplies
48 - 52 rue montmartre. corner rue etienne marcel. metro 4: les halles.
33 (0) 1 42 33 71 65 www.asimon.fr
mon 1:30 - 6:30p tue - fri 9a - 6:30p sat 9:30a - 6:30p

opened in 1884. owners: the pillivuyt family
visa. mc

Of all the common fantasies of fleeing one's humdrum life, moving to Paris and opening a charming little café has got to be one of the most desirable. Pouring glasses of Ricard for handsome *madames* and *monsieurs* sounds infinitely more appealing than analyzing forecast charts in Des Moines, doesn't it? Well dear, disgruntled workers, *a. simon* is the first step to your new exciting life. At this Parisian institution, you will find all the necessary equipment to open said fantasy café or bistro. There is nothing really stopping you now as *a. simon* is open six days a week. Hop to it.

covet:
gite a paté oval dish
enameled round address numbers
sausage stuffer
crêpe iron cleaning brush
frites cutter
printed linen dish towels
chef coats
round orielles porcelain dishes

avenches

singularly artistic jewelry

17 rue de poitou. corner of rue debelleyme. metro 8: filles du calvaire
33 (0) 1 42 72 81 73 www.avenches-paris.com
tue - sat noon - 7p

opened in 2009. owner: vincent vaucher
all major credit cards accepted
custom orders / design

3rd arr >

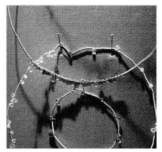

Over the years I have worked on these guides I have come across a few artisans whose work has so impressed me, I felt like a talent agent seeing the young Meryl Streep in an early performance. Jewelry maker Vincent Vaucher is such a find. His miniscule Marais shop, *Avenches*, is a singular vision of an artist whose aesthetic stradles vulnerability and elegance. His pieces are made with exquisite craftsmanship and luxurious, yet understated materials. I had to restrain my wanton enthusiasm so as not to destroy the perfect, serene mood here. He is one to watch.

covet:
coiled chain & precious stone necklaces
coiled silver wire & stone bracelets
coiled wire rings
gold lip brooch
gold & thread chains
gold comb pin
black pearl earrings
wire eye pins

balouga

modern furniture for children

25 rue des filles du calvaire. between boulevard du temple and rue de turenne
metro 8: filles du calvaire
33 (0) 1 42 74 01 49 www.balouga.com
tue - fri 12:30 - 7p sat 2 - 7p

opened in 2006. owner: véronique cota
visa. mc
online shopping

3rd arr >

Sophisticated parents often try to influence their kids to make elevated choices. This only leads to disappointment when the little cherub chooses a Bratz doll and names it "Sweet Princess of the Pinkland Dreams." The moral here: let your offspring figure some stuff out on their own. However, parents can make decisions that will leave a lasting impression. Furnishing his/her room with wee-sized design classics from *Balouga* is a primer to the world of good design. Kids may not realize they are being influenced, but will be happy down the road when they have outgrown fairyland chic.

covet:
balouga edition furniture
miller goodman shape maker
string swedish shelving
lunatic desk system
meridiana cuckoo clock
reproduction eames furniture for kids
kazam desk
le corbusier modular

bda

fabulous vintage
46 rue la condamine. corner of rue nollet. metro 13: la fourche
33 (0) 1 42 93 54 70 www.bastiendealmeida.com
tue - sat 11a - 8p

opened in 2009. owner: bastien de almeida
all major credit cards accepted
sewing classes

17th arr >  **s05**

The French do everything with a little more flair than we do. They do not send a dozen roses for a birthday, they send four dozen roses. Where our vintage stores often look like messy, moldering closets, Parisien vintage stores are incredible, like Bastien's shop *BDA*. This place razzles and dazzles, with vintage gowns and dresses displayed in a club-like atmosphere. And though he's fond of a brand-name label, he cares more about what's beautiful, pointing to a gown displayed under a stuffed ostrich. An excellent example of where more is more.

covet:
pedro rodriguez sequined number
excentriques book
cabaret book
the house of nine
'80s geometric sheath dress
goatskin coat
wigs done up in old styles
leigh bowery dvd

calourette

tempting accessories
27 rue du bourg-tibourg
between rue de la verrerie and rue sainte-croix de la bretonnerie
metro 1 / 11: hôtel de ville
33 (0) 1 48 04 08 25 www.calourette.com
tue - sun 2 - 7:30p

opened in 2007. owner: marianne rautureau
visa. mc
online shopping

4th arr > **s06**

Some people are pulled together; others not. I don't think I am, but I am beginning to understand how to do it. What I mean is that certain people can throw on jeans and a t-shirt, clean or dirty, add a necklace, and they look amazing. So I've figured out that a necklace, or a hat, or a scarf, mixed with a cup of self confidence makes it all work. *Calourette* would be a good place to start adding accessories esteem. This shop is filled with fun extras made by Marianne or sourced by her. She's got "it," and with a few more adornments, I hope to have "it," too.

covet:
calourette jewelry
schmoove
bernstock speirs hats
agnelle gloves
tricolore t's
babbu scarves
spring court shoes
camo sweaters

cartes postales anciennes

antique postcards from exotic places

50 passage des panoramas. between boulevard poissonnière and rue saint-marc
metro 8 / 9: grand boulevards
33 (0) 1 42 33 49 95
mon - sat 10a - 6:30p

opened in 2000. owner: prins patrick
visa. mc

These days, everything is in transition, and many things we once thought were rock solid are just hollow facades (Bernie Madoff, Tiger Woods). Not to get too serious, but the times have me reflecting. This might be why I became transfixed at the antique postcard shops in the Passage Panorama. My favorite is *Cartes Postales Anciennes*. No beach babes holding brewskies on cards here, but rather cards sent long ago from travels to Turkey, Iran, India—when the written word was revered. The glimpse back at this pre-digital era feels poignant, like a hint at forgotten wisdom, or a much-needed escape from reality.

covet:
a sampling of postcard categories:
  afrique du sud
  moroc
  italie
  napoleon
  la seine
  the sea
  oddities

chi.ind

paris designer of sassy tops for women

117 rue vieille du temple. between rue du perche and rue debelleyme
metro 8: filles du calvaire
33 (0) 1 42 74 05 70
tue - sat 11a - 2p, 3 - 7:30p sun - mon 2 - 7:30p

opened in 2006. owner: david chemla
all major credit cards accepted

3rd arr > **s08**

Plopping down in a city for a long period is great fun. You really get to know a place when stationed there for weeks, or months! I have discovered a downside however. Not unlike a runner hitting "the wall," I sometimes will wake up and think, I can't bear to wear this ratty old sweater one more day. If I were a girl having that type of day, I'd go to *chi.ind*. Designed and sewn in-house, the sassy tops here are fun, beautifully made and reasonably priced. Replicas of men's oxford shirts with a young, sexy-girl silhouette could become such a fave, you might ditch your old duds altogether.

covet:
chi.ind shirts:
  grace
  geny
  coco striped & ruffled
  douard men's style
luce jumpsuit
fred cashmere sweater
gaby overcoat

cire trudon

the oldest candle maker in france

78 rue de seine. between rue saint-sulpice and rue lobineau
metro 4: saint-germain-des-prés
33 (0) 1 43 26 46 50 www.ciretrudon.com
mon - sat 10a - 7p

opened in 1643. owners: the blondeau family
all major credit cards accepted

6th arr > **s09**

Cire Trudon was originally founded in 1643 and is the oldest manufacturer of candles in France. Within this long history, a highlight was supplying all of the candles to Versaille under Louis XVI. Though these candles were to provide light, I like to imagine ol' Louis sitting around in some silken, royal loungewear, listening to light jazz, with a *Trudon* candle pleasingly filling the room with scents of tuberose or vetiver. The shop has an amazing history and today offers candles of all shapes, scents and sizes. A perfect souvenir to take back to your own 10,000-acre country estate.

covet:
scented candles:
  carmalite
  revolution
  trianon
  abd el kader
candle busts:
  napoléon
  marie antoinette

comptoir des écritures

beautiful equipment for writing

35 rue quincampoix. between rue berger and rue rambuteau
metro 3: rambuteau
33 (0) 1 42 78 95 10 www.comptoirdesecritures.com
tue - fri 11a - 7p sat 11a - 6p

opened in 1999. owner: lolita becerril
visa. mc
online shopping

4th arr >

I have a befuddling disconnect in accordance to expensive things. I'm the opposite of a crow—I will stop to pick up a piece of twine while ignoring a five-carat diamond next to it. This is why *Comptoir des Écritures*, a shop selling Asian inks and papers for calligraphers, makes me melt into a puddle of goo. Stacks of oatmeal-colored handmade paper—perfectly proportioned and precisely stacked on a golden wooden tray—are far better than the Hope diamond in my mind. Everything here is so considered and beautiful, yet made of such common materials. This is like heaven for us non-crows.

covet:
le papier by lucien polastron
raw pigments
handmade writing paper
calligraphy postcards
handmade books
zeichentusche inks
calligraphy brushes
quills

deyrolle

a paris institution, open once again!

46 rue du bac. between boulevard saint-germain and rue de l'université

metro 12: rue du bac

33 (0) 1 42 22 30 07 www.deyrolle.fr

mon 10a - 1p, 2 - 7p tue - sat 10a - 7p

opened in 1831. owner: prince louis-albert de broglie

visa. mc

7th arr >

Sometimes a terrible event happens, and your friends think of you immediately. This happened recently when Bea Arthur died. My Facebook wall went crazy with condolences. Equally as grave was when a fire struck the mythical taxidermy world of *Deyrolle*. For years, I have been proselytizing about this place's ability to command wonder from anyone lucky enough to visit its storied rooms. The day of the fire, dozens of friends reached out, stunned. I'm happy to report that *Deyrolle* has reopened and maintains the same glorious fascination it has always had. A phoenix rises.

covet:
framed & mounted exotic butterflies
french elementary school maps
taxidermied giraffe
seashells & coral
le prince jardinier candles
bird eggs
great selection of gardening snips
taxidermied chickens

farida

men's and women's self-assured fashions
61 rue charlot. corner of rue du forez. metro 8: filles du calvaire
33 (0) 1 42 78 71 09
tue - sat 11a - 8p sun 2 - 7p

opened in 2008. owner: farida senooci
all major credit cards accepted

3rd arr >

If the fashion continuum ranges from 1 (Jill Sander white shirts) to 10 (Lacroix couture), my wardrobe is filled with 3s. Wearing boring buttondowns and chinos with the occasional sport coat thrown on should disqualify me from doing this job. Even though I am a 3 dresser, nothing makes me happier than the numbers over 5. Farida, a former stylist, has an eye for clothing and accessories with panache. With a large selection of Vivienne Westwood, here is fashion at its most creative—pieces that show outrageous can also be tasteful. Memo to self: incorporate more animal prints into my wardrobe.

covet:
vivienne westwood
opening ceremony
heal
carven
0044
david szeto
jas mb
eley kishimoto

french touche

french-made objects

1 rue jacquemont. corner of avenue de clichy. metro 13: la fourche
33 (0) 1 42 63 31 36 www.frenchtouche.com
tue - fri 1p - 8p sat 11a - 8p

opened in 2002. owner: valérie fleurent-didier
visa. mc
online shopping.

17th arr >

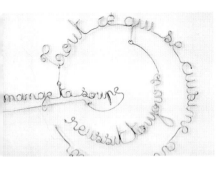

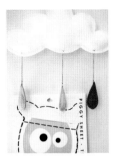

The act of making things and selling them is a core component to an economy. This remains true in Paris where tiny shops exist doing work as simple as chair caning or leather bookbinding. It's reassuring to see this tradition continuing at *French Touche*. This eensy shop features works by talented artisans from around France, all partaking in the simple act of making something and selling it. From jewelry and handbags to mobiles and lighting, the range is wide and creative. What is consistent is the joy of knowing your purchase keeps the cogs turning in this artistic world.

covet:
voici, voila, voilou magazine
claire hacquet-chaut jewelry
alpha beta
one bag one
estelle cusset cloches
velvet marmelade kids' clothing
marinettechou wire sculpture
les bons baisers booklets

french trotters

clothing for men

116 rue vieille du temple. corner of rue debelleyme. metro 8: saint-sébastien froissart
30 rue de charonne. between rue taillandiers and ledru rollin. metro 8: ledru rollin
33 (0) 1 44 61 00 14 www.frenchtrotters.fr
tue - sat 11a - 7:30p sun - mon 2:30 - 7:30p

opened in 2008. owners: clarent and carole dehlouz
all major credit cards accepted

3rd arr > s14

I met the *French Trotters* duo Clarent and Carole while working on the first edition of this book. At the time, I had to stifle my *Talented Mr. Ripley* urges, fantasizing how I could take over their enviable life of travel. A rare moment of good judgment kept me from pursuing this desire, allowing the duo to prosper, opening a new menswear shop. Their discriminating taste and restrained style once again garnered critical acclaim. As I checked out the offerings at this new store, I felt the familiar jealousy return, and I found myself muttering under my breath, *"Je m'appelle Clarent."*

covet:
vintage casio watches
mismo bags
commune de paris
b store
volta
libertine - libertine
gitman brothers ties
opening ceremony

ie boutique

every day objects and kids clothing from india
128 rue vieille du temple. between rue de turenne and rue pastourelle
metro 8: filles du calvaire
33 (0) 1 44 59 87 72 www.ieboutique.com
tue - sun 11a - 8p

opened in 2003. owner: durgué laigret
visa. mc

3rd arr > **s15**

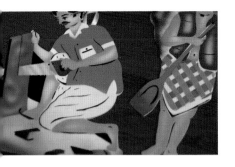

One of my great joys when it comes to travelling is bringing home mundane, everyday objects from the countries I visit. For example: my beloved French stapler—every time I use it, I smile, thinking about my fantastic trip. The wares at *ie boutique* are all everyday objects that one would find in India, and though they are ubiqutous in that part of the world, they are worlds away from being mundane. There's everything from buttons to Indian Barbie—which is far more exotic and cool then, say, Palm Beach Swim Suit Barbie.

covet:
indian cut out figures
antique bells
colorful printed cotton yardage
clothing for kids made from imported cotton
indian buttons
children's books from india
indian barbie
colorful slippers

isaac reina

leather goods for men and women
38 rue de sévigné. between rue du parc royal and rue des francs bourgeois
metro 8: chemin vert
33 (0) 1 42 78 81 95 www.isaacreina.com
tue - sat 11a - 7:30p

opened in 2006. owner: isaac reina
visa. mc

3rd arr > s16

A minimalist painter friend of mine drives me crazy, spending days deciding where to make the faintest mark to finish a work. I want to scream, "Loosen up." But in looking at *Isaac Reina's* exquisite leather bags and accessories, it's clear to me that spending the time to get your work exactly right pays off. Having designed accessories for Hermès and M. Margiela, Mr. Reina has a golden provenance, and his buttery leathers are perfect: in proportion, in craftsmanship, in their utilitarian elegance. Isaac's leather pieces prove that minimalism can be masterful.

covet:
magic box necessaire
014 sac 48h standard
043 sac 24h
144 for make up soft pouch
148 magic trotter bag
150 petit sac pillow
160 porte feuilles "classify"
161 porte documents "classify"

kitsuné

art, music and fashion all-in-one
52 rue richelieu. corner of rue des petits champs
metro 1: palais royal-musée du louvre
33 (0) 1 42 60 34 28 www.kitsune.fr
tue - sat 11a - 7:30p

opened in 2008. owners: masaya kuroki and gildas loaec
all major credit cards accepted

1st arr >

One of the reasons I didn't become a fashion designer is my addiction to sweatpants. You see, one has to be 100% committed to fashion to have one's designs taken seriously, and I can not live without my elastic-waisted, fuzzy pants. This is not to say I don't love wearing nice clothes, though. I'd wear about anything from *Kitsuné*, a Paris-based design house headed by a stylish designer/dj duo. Silhouettes are part preppy, part Japanese arty—these clothes are as cool as their originators. I think of *Kitsuné* as the warm-up wear to my cozy pants.

covet:
kitsuné:
   white button shirt with black piping
   navy-inspired cable knit sweater
   red, white & blue western-inspired shirt
   pierre hardy collaboration shoes
   dj mixed cds
   red ankle boots
   great t's

135

kyrie eleison

modern clothing for women
15 carrefour de l'odéon. corner of rue monsieur le prince. metro 4: odéon
33 (0) 1 46 34 26 91
tue - sat 10:30a - 7:30p sun 2 - 6p

opened in 2007. owner: zoe ferdinand
all major credit cards accepted

6th arr >

The other day I ran into an old college friend. It was great to see her until she noted my shirt and said, "It's funny, I remember that shirt from college." I realized with horror that the shirt had been worn through both the Clinton and the Bush administrations. I promptly burned it. If your closet is filled with clothes you danced to Cyndi Lauper in, perhaps you should visit *Kyrie Eleison*, where you can find clothing and accessories from emerging designers. You can't deny having lived through the Hammer Pants era, but with *Kyrie Eleison* you no longer have to wear them.

covet:
virginie castaway
cacheral
stella nova
le mont st. michel
erotokritos
yumi
ambali
gaspard yurkievich

la fille du pirate

nautical antiques and miniatures

2 place du palais royal. corner rue valois. metro 1: palais royal-musée du louvre
33 (0) 1 42 60 20 30 www.lafilledupirate.com
tue - sun 11a - 7p

opened in 1986. owner: marie-noëlle dieutegard
visa. mc

1st arr >

I felt like I'd discovered the land of miniature people, Lilliput, entering *La Fille du Pirate*. This amazing shop, near the Louvre, offers all things nautical but specializes in miniature antique replicas of seagoing vessels. These museum-quality models are incredible. The impeccable craftsmanship scales all the way down to miniature- sized ropes operating wee-sized sails as if they were actual, full-sized ships. I asked the shopkeeper if he would tie me up, so I could pretend to be Gulliver awaking in Lilliput. Perhaps I used the wrong French words for tie me up, as he politely declined and asked me to leave.

covet:
incredible replicas of sailing ships
sextants
scrimshawed whalebone
antique globes
looking glasses
porthole windows
nautical-themed oil paintings
planetary orbit models

la galerie végétale

art and flora

29 rue des vinaigriers. between quai de valmy and rue lucien sampaix
metro 5: jacques bonsargent
33 (0) 1 40 37 07 16 www.lagalerievegetale.com
tue - thu 10a - 2p, 3 - 7p fri - sun 10a - 2p, 3 - 8p

opened in 2006. owners: solveig kuffer and michel lebreton
all major credit cards accepted

10th arr > **s20**

When I shop with friends, they seem to resent my job with the *eat.shop* guides. If we are in a store that doesn't quite pass muster, I will mention my favorite equivalent in another city. They think I'm jaded—I think I'm worldly. Regardless, it's impressive when I see a store doing something completely unique. Such is the case at La *Galerie Végétale*. Part flower shop, part art gallery—this warehouse space changes drastically and regularly, so each visit is a fresh and wonderful experience. Beware friends, I have something to name drop next time we're out and about.

covet:
succulents
cut flowers
orchids
rubber satchels
day of the dead masks
piñatas
recycled furniture
housemade candles

le bouclard

avant fashion

15 rue charlot. corner rue pastourelle. metro 8: filles du calvaire
33 (0) 1 42 36 14 66 www.le-bouclard.com
tue - sat 1 - 7:30p

opened in 2006. owner: cecile audouin
all major credit cards accepted
online shopping

3rd arr > **s21**

Paris can be intimidating. Between the historicalness of it all and the chicness everywhere you look, it's easy to feel like the country mouse. At *Le Bouclard*, my hick-o-meter flared. Feeling nervous, I picked up a gorgeous shoe, acting like I was thinking of trying it on. Owner Cecile said, "I don't think that will fit you—it's for a woman." I laughed. She laughed. At that moment I knew that there was no reason to be intimidated. Though she's a Parisian and I'm an Oregonian, we both shared the same interest—an appreciation of beautiful things.

covet:
final home
vans by volt
sns herning
rick owens for eastpak
tsumori chisato
le bouclard brand
cabane de zucca
artysm

le jeune frères

hardware for the home

209 rue du faubourg saint-antoine. between rue saint-bernard and rue faidherbe
metro 8: faidherbe-chaligny
33 (0) 1 43 72 99 26 www.lejeunefreres.com
mon - fri 9a - noon, 2 - 6p sat 9a - noon, 2 - 5p

opened in 1941. owner: aranha habelous
visa. mc
online shopping

11th arr >  **s22**

Are there others like me? I ask myself this when I travel and obsess over all the utilitarian details I see. I'm positive no one else opens a café door over and over again, watching the way the latch snaps back by the simple action of a handsome spring. And I am sure that stopping in one's tracks to caress the latch of a Metro door, gauging the substantial and satisfying weight, is clearly certifiable. If others like me do exist, I suggest *Le Jeune Frères*, where you will get lost in the jumble of drawers storing everything from house numbers to light switches. It's a place with beautiful things for weirdos like me.

covet:
brass house numbers
cool cabinet pulls
casement window hardware
ornate keyholes
brass latches
lion door knockers
coat & hat hooks
door plaques

les vélos parisiens

cool bicycles and accessories

3 rue de l'abbé grégoire. between rue de sèvres and rue du cherche-midi
metro 10: vaneau
33 (0) 1 45 44 72 97 www.lesvelosparisiens.com
tue 10a - 1p, 2:30 - 7p wed 10a - 4p thu - sat 10a - 1p, 2:30 - 7p

opened in 1997. owner: sebastien reboux
visa. mc
repairs / service

6th arr > **s23**

With the new Vélib system of rentable bikes throughout Paris, it couldn't be cooler to cycle. One problem, though, is that our stupid American credit cards, without smart chips, won't work in some of the machines. Hrmph. You can still rent a bike elsewhere in the city, but I highly suggest buying one at *Les Vélos Parisiens,* where they specialize in unusual bicycles. A pack of foldable bikes greets you as a reminder of how darn easy it would be to take one of these babies out of town for a country excursion—your own tour de France.

covet:
brompton folding bikes
yakkay helmets
brookes saddles
early rider wooden bikes
les vélos parisiens leather bags
nutcase helmets
sacoches de velo bags
kusua

l'objet

beautiful objects for the home

9 rue des francs-bourgeois. between rue de sèvigne and rue de turenne
metro 1: saint paul
33 (0) 1 42 72 43 22
tue - sat 11a - 7p sun 2 - 6:30p

opened in 1990. owner: laure jouannigot
visa. mc

4th arr > **s24**

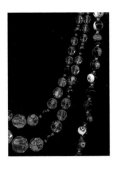

This is a lesson in simply opening your eyes. While in Paris I was looking to find a large silver serving spoon as the antique flatware available there is so superior to anything we have. In the Marais, I found myself on Rue des Francs-Bourgeois, the main drag that I have walked down hundreds of times. Almost by accident I swerved into *L'Objet*, an antiques store I'd seen for years but had somehow ignored because of its location amongst big international stores. To my surprise, the shop was great—and there was my spoon, perfect and affordable. Plain as the nose on my face.

covet:
silver serving spoon by christophe
etched antique juice glasses
antique id bracelets
hand-painted peacock serving plate
antique glass beads
antique salt & pepper wells
baroque candlesticks
silver cups

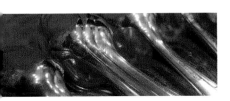

maison francis kurkdjian

paris perfumerie

5 rue d'alger. between rue de rivoli and rue du mont thabor. metro 1: tuileries
33 (0) 42 60 07 07 www.franciskurkdjian.com
mon - fri 11a - 1:30p, 2:30 - 7p sat 11a - 7p

opened in 2009. owner: francis kurkdjian
all major credit cards accepted
online shopping. custom scents

1st arr >

Remember back when you would buy a perfume in Paris because it was a unique souvenir? This is an old-fashioned notion because fragrances have become ubiquitous, duty-free schlock. *Maison Francis Kurkdjian* revives the conviction that a French perfume is a distinct and romantic embodiment of this city. Francis has made scents for many of the big French couture houses. Now, under his own name, he offers fragrances in both day and evening varieties, and you can even have a signature scent made by appointment. Save your duty-free dollars for giant Toblerone bars.

covet:
eau de parfum:
  lumière noire
  apom
  saqua universalis
papiers encens
le bracelet parfumé
les bulles d'agathe cut herbs
parfums d'intérieur

maison jean-baptiste

accessories for men

155 rue amelot. near boulevard voltaire. metro 3 / 5 / 8 / 9 / 11: république
33 (0) 1 78 56 58 72 www.maisonjeanbaptiste.com
tue - sat 11:30a - 1:30p, 2:30 - 7:30p

opened in 2008. owner: jean-baptiste
all major credit cards accepted

11th arr >

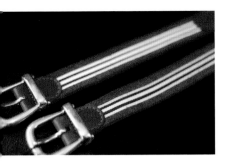

Being a child of the '70s, I'm a big supporter of women's lib. And there's no doubt that there are some pretty powerful ladies calling the shots around the world right now. But what about men's rights? Like a man's right to accessorize. I would say that *Maison Jean-Baptiste,* which specializes in modern, urban men's shoes and accessories, is helping equalize the playing field when it comes to fashion extras. These luxuries are not just for women anymore. Men have just as much right to accessorize to their heart's content. Jean-Baptiste, you are a leader in men's lib.

covet:
baptiste viry cuffs
superfuture sunglasses
happy socks
florian denicourt bags & shoes
alessandro dell'acqua shoes
superga shoes
roberto collina scarves
michael guérisse o'leary

mamie gâteaux brocante

antique shop owned by the mamie gâteaux people
68 rue du cherche-midi. between rue de l'abbé grégoire and rue jean ferrandi
metro 4: saint-placide
33 (0) 1 45 44 36 63 www.mamie-gateaux.com
tue - sat 11:30a - 6p (if closed ask at the salon de thé)

opened in 2005. owners: hervé and mariko duplessis
cash only

6th arr >

Don't get me wrong—I love a good Louis the XIV armoire, but I doubt I will ever be able to afford one. Nor is my house a baroque castle. Certain antiques seem to be for royalty or owners of software companies, but I prefer something a little more accessible that I can find at the *brocante* **(antique market)** run by the folks from *Mamie Gâteaux*. When two storefronts became available next to their *salon de thé*, they decided to sell the type of goods that decorate their restaurant—items ranging from cookware to French primary school maps and lesson books. Here's to the little people!

covet:
antique camera obscura
vintage maps & posters
heavy french linens
vintage cooking utensils
olds wooden toys
café au lait bowls
antique clock
antique french advertising

marché aux puces de saint-oeun clignancourt

granddaddy of all paris flea markets

140 rue des rosiers. metro 4: clingnancourt
33 (0) 1 40 12 32 58 www.parispuces.com/en
sat 9a - 6p sun 10a - 6p mon 11a - 5p

opened in 1885
all major credit cards accepted

18th arr > **s28**

This grandaddy of Paris flea markets is most commonly referred to by its metro stop: *Clingnancourt*. You absolutely must visit here, but go with perseverance. Climbing the stairs out of the metro can feel like a sea of confusion. Follow the throngs past the vendors selling fake designer bags and rasta hats, and you will be rewarded. Hall after hall of diverse and astounding antiques provide mostly a window-shopping experience unless you are in the market for a hotel-lobby-scaled chandelier. The splendor being peddled here is beyond your wildest dreams. But who knows? A special trinket may be within your grasp.

covet:
stalls within the market:
  biron
  paul bert
  serpette
  cambo
  dauphine
  l'entrepôt
  jules vallès

noir kennedy

youthful rocker style

12 and 22 rue du roi de sicile. corner of rue pavée. metro 1: saint paul
33 (0) 1 42 71 15 50 www.noirkennedy.fr
mon 1 - 8p tue - sat 11a - 8p sun 2 - 8p

opened in 2008
visa. mc

4th arr > **s29**

One of my all-time, top-five ways to let loose is driving in the car alone, singing at top volume to my favorite music. This is my way of living out a fantasy persona which has me as the lead singer of Bauhaus. I feel a bit wimpy that I've never come out of my goth rock closet. Maybe if I were younger I would and I'd shop at *Noir Kennedy*. I'd find everything here for my secret fantasy life from super-tight skinny jeans to vintage wingtips. The style here is a touch rockabilly mixed with goth. On the whole, it's all about rocker attitude. Just like me when I'm driving in my Volkswagen.

covet:
noir kennedy printed t's
vintage vans
vintage americana clothing
noir kennedy jeans
vintage wing tips
french foreign legion jackets
cheap monday
bowler hats

norden

scandinavian-designed men's and women's clothing

5 rue commines. corner of rue froissart. metro 8: filles du calvaire
33 (0) 1 42 74 82 01 www.ilovenorden.com
tue - sat 11a - 7p sun 2 - 6p

opened in 2008. owners: hannah and eric delafosse
visa. mc

3rd arr > **s30**

Living in Scandinavia would have some serious benefits: amazing quality of life, scorchingly attractive people and an appreciation for good design. The downsides: seven months with no sun, too much reindeer on the menu and temperatures appropriate for said reindeer. Fortunately the charms of Scandinavia have caught on and are available in warmer climes. *Norden* features clothing, furniture and objects all from the land of the midnight sun. And the good news is you don't have to eat a Rudolph burger to get them.

covet:
wood wood
our legacy
permanent vacation
gram shoes
vintage scandinavian teak furniture
swedish cinema posters
peter jensen
sns

objet sonore

incredible vintage stereo equipment
19 rue debelleyme. between rue du poitou and rue de bretagne
metro 8: filles du calvaire
33 (0) 9 50 48 34 18 www.presence-audio.com
tue - sat 10:30a - 7:30p

opened in 2008. owner: luca minchillo
all major credit cards accepted
online shopping

3rd arr > **s31**

I am willing to be a total nerd when it comes to certain things. Vintage stereo equipment makes me wave my geek flag high. The combination of superior technology and stellar '60s and '70s design is a total bull's-eye into awesometown. I'd fill every room in my house with one of these masterpieces if I won the lottery, and then I'd buy two more houses and fill them up. I'd say *Objet Sonore* is almost too good to be true. Vintage Braun designs by Dieter Rams next to pristine Bang & Olufsen turntables—I feel my heart palpitating.

covet:
vintage stereo equipment:
  marantz
  braun
  technics
  thorens
  bang & olufsen
  grundig
  brion vega

papier+

handmade journals and paper goods

9 rue du pont louis-phillippe. between rue françois miron and quai de l'hôtel de ville
metro 1: saint paul
33 (0) 1 42 77 70 49 www.papierplus.com
mon - sat noon - 7p

opened in 1976. owner: denis bruner
visa. mc
online shopping

4th arr > **s32**

One to follow tradition, I looked up a list of gifts I should give on certain occasions. There I found that the first wedding anniversary is about giving paper. My first thought was what a disappointment to get the good stuff in the first year. Who cares about silver, which requires 25 years of matrimony? Obviously I love fine paper and stationery. This is why *Papier+* resonates with me so. I look at the beautiful binders and journals, carefully crafted, and I am moved by the potential creativity. And when I see the careful placement given to a stack of fine writing paper, I realize I'm not the only one who cares about paper.

covet:
presentation boxes
artist's portfolios
binders
colored stationery
photo albums with window
press books
autograph books
journals

petit pan

magical children's decor and furnishings

39 rue françois miron. between rue de fourcy and rue tiron. metro 1: saint paul
7 rue de prague. corner rue emilio castelar. metro 1 / 5 / 8: ledru rollins
33 (0) 1 44 54 90 84 www.petitpan.com
tue - sat 10:30a - 2p, 3 - 7:30p

opened in 2004. owner: myriam
visa. mc

4th arr > s33

Petit Pan thrust me into the children's world of make believe. Full-size busts of polar bears and larger than life butterflies meticulously hand made of painted silk and bamboo, illuminate the walls and ceilings like a friendly, cartoon-like episode of *Wild Kingdom*. I swear I could hear the sound of banjos playing "The Country Bear Jamboree" as I entered the animated vignette of a campfire complete with water boiling in a cooking pot. I felt like i was taking a mini safari into the owner's imagination, with thankfully no worries about a stampede.

covet:
silk duck kites
bamboo & silk lanterns
guirlande étoiles
mushroom mobiles
garland fêtes
brio toys
kid quilts
gouache

pigalle

men's and women's fashions

7 rue henry monnier. between rue notre dame and rue de navarin. metro 12: pigalle
33 (0) 1 48 78 59 74 www.pigalleparis.com
tue - sat noon - 8p sun 2 - 8p

opened in 2008. owners: doushka and stephane ashpool
visa. mc

9th arr > **s34**

When you look through the pages of French Vogue, it is easy to forget how hard it is to make the outfits look great. Mixing and matching clothes is easy, if you are Grace Coddington, where lesser stylists just end up making a mess. At the new boutique *Pigalle*, the style within made me stand up and take notice. Run by a mother and son team, they mix haute and street, couture and sporty in a totally seamless, super chic way. So even if you aren't Rachel Zoe, no worries. The team at *Pigalle* has already done the hard work for you; just relax and buy.

covet:
wood wood
dries van noten
phenomenon
ann demeulemeester
rick owens
sharon wauchob
gustavolins
manish arora

plagg

young, cool scandinavian designs for her
41 rue charlot. corner of rue de bretegne. metro 3 / 5 / 8 / 9 / 11: république
33 (0) 1 42 78 37 60
tue - sat 11a - 8p sun 2 - 7:30p

opened in 2006. owner: barbara kurdziel
visa. mc

3rd arr > s35

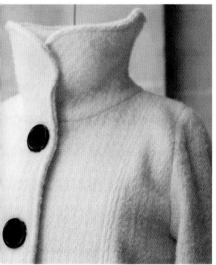

I know I talk about my love of Sweden a lot. Here's my justification. Sweden's population is about 9 million people, close to the tally for New Jersey. Yet this lovely Nordic land has produced Acne jeans, Abba and the Swedish Chef, to name just a few. From New Jersey we get Snooki and the Cake Boss. Get my point? What's cool about *Plagg* is that Barbara carries the lines of many young, not-fully-discovered Swedish designers. These pieces convey a casual coolness—laid-back yet somehow pulled together. I'm thinking there should be a reality show called "Stylish People from Sweden. "

covet:
designers remix collection
burfitt
mini market
stine goya
camilla norrback
karine arabian
beck sondergaard

pop market

just for fun objects
50 rue bichat. between quai de jemmapes and rue de la grange aux belles
metro 4 / 5 / 7: gare de l'est
33 (0) 9 52 79 96 86 www.popmarket.free.fr
tue - sat 10:30a - 7:30p sun 2 - 7p

opened in 2009. owners: céline fishetti and marion thomassin
visa. mc

10th arr >

One of my favorite mini-memories of working on this book took place at *Pop Market*. I was busy taking pictures when I saw two policemen walking in. Minutes later, I found myself near them as they were looking at models of American cop cars from the '50s. They found them incredibly hilarious and began to laugh. I chuckled too, laughing at them laughing. Then the train left the station as laughter built to a hilarious conclusion with tears running down our faces and one of them purchasing a model. No words were exchanged during this encounter. Names were changed to protect the innocent.

covet:
anne claire petit knit sack
ah, quel plaisir
mark's notebooks
baker backpack
birthday bunting
tater pots
extratapete murals
abc du père castors

serendipity

furnishings for kids that make you happy
81 - 83 rue du cherche-midi. corner of rue jean ferrandi. metro 4: saint-placide
33 (0) 1 40 46 01 15 www.serendipity.fr
tue - sat 11a - 7p

opened in 2009. owners: elisa de bartillat and laurence simoncini
visa. mc

6th arr > **s37**

Life is full of times when you work hard to make something happen, like pursuing a coveted new job or working off some holiday pounds. Then there are times when an awesome gift falls out of nowhere: a snowstorm cancels your dental appointment or an incredible bistro opens a block from your house. These are serendipitous events and make life a little sweeter. *Serendipity,* the store, is filled with objects that make you happy in this way. Playful items for kids are not only beautifully designed but have a lighthearted take on childhood—and no luck is required to enjoy them.

covet:
baladeuse lamp
wool balls
antique desk lamps
cool, industrial kids' beds
kid-sized adirondack chairs
wire wastebackets
felt birdhouse
white wooden toy bulldozer

175

si tu veux

good old-fashioned toy shop
68 galerie vivienne. near rue vivienne. metro 3: bourse
33 (0) 1 42 60 59 97 www.galerie-vivienne.com
tue - sat 10a - 7p

opened in 1976. owner: madeleine deny
visa. mc

2nd arr >

It is impossible for me to fathom being raised in Paris. It's got to be so different from the way I was raised in the middle of America. For example, the idea of being a kid and getting to choose a holiday gift at *Si Tu Veux* is enthralling compared to my own experience going to Christmasland at the local Farm and Fleet. The game I used to plead for, 'Hungry, Hungry Hippos,' pales in comparison to the build-your-own chateaux kit I saw here. Who knows? Maybe you get blasé about chateaus when you are around them all of the time, but it would be fun to be a kid again, living in Paris to find out.

covet:
paper swords
rope ring toss
marble run
goki football game
chateau building blocks
crazy campers game
"c'est moi le plus beau" book
mikado giant

spree

the perfect store
16 rue la vieuville. between rue des abbesses and rue des trois frères
metro 12: abbesses
33 (0) 1 42 23 41 40 www.spree.fr
mon 2 - 7p tue - sat 11a - 7:30p

opened in 2001. owners: roberta oprandi and bruno hadjadj
visa. mc

18th arr >

In order for a business to be featured for a second time in this book, they had to do something extraordinary like opening a killer new location, burn down and reopen with the same intangible magic as before or be *Spree*. This place is *fantastique*, like two stores wrapped up in one: a inspired clothing store offering tightly curated young and stylish options, and an exceptional collection of vintage furniture, with offerings rivalling the best of mid-to-late century, vintage furniture shops anywhere. *French Trotters*, *Deyrolle* and *Spree:* you're an elite group.

covet:
isabel marant
marc by marc jacobs
il by saori komatsu
vannessa bruno bags
spree shoes
apc
jo colombo lamp
great vintage furniture

179

surface to air

hip, young clothing and accessories

108 rue vieille du temple. corner of rue debelleyme. metro 8: filles du calvaire
33 (0) 1 44 61 76 27 www.surfacetoair.com
tue - sat 11a - 7:30p

opened in 2000. owners: paris based collective
all major credit cards accepted
online shopping

3rd arr >

When in Paris, I love it when I appear so "with it" that someone will ask me for directions. One day a couple of American hipsters asked me where to find *The Surface of Air*. I rolled my eyes that they mangled the name of this Parisian art, design and fashion institution. I mustered a fake French accent and sent them off to Rue Charlot. I was feeling quite proud of myself until later that day when I went to *Surface to Air* to take pictures for this book, only to find it gone. It had recently moved into a new flagship shop on a different street. So much for Mr. Know-It-All.

covet:
trap jaw pendant
three finger rings
dotty skirt
men's shawl cardigan
claude classic shirt
edward lace boots
buckle ankle boot
trefix dress

talc

children's fashions

7 rue des quatre vents. between rue de condé and rue de seine. metro 4: odéon
60 rue de saintonge. corner of rue de turenne. metro 8: filles du calvaire
33 (0) 1 42 77 52 63 www.talcboutique.com
mon 2 - 7p tue - sat 11a - 7p

opened in 2007. owner: catherine chobas
visa. mc

6th arr / 3rd arr > s41

Why are the French so stylish? Because they have awesome kids' clothing stores. If you start cultivating the basics of style to a toddler, it's ingrained in them by the time they start dating. *Talc* starts kids early, offering clothes from three months and up, focusing on a cultivated but casual look. Think peacoats and printed cotton button-down shirts. These are mix-and-match classics, sophisticated yet carefree enough to give little Yves a look worthy of an art gallery opening by way of the playground. Well, that question is answered. Next up: Why does France have such delicious cheese?

covet:
robe louvre rivoli
sweat république
burnou pull
short raspail
bilet luxembourg
blouse tuilleries
robe saint sulpice
rabbit hair / wool hat

tremblay alvergne

preppy yet hip men's clothing

11 rue du perche. between rue charlot and rue vieille du temple
metro 8: filles du calvaire
33 (0) 1 42 74 15 35 www.tremblay-alvergne.com
tue - sat 11:30a - 7:30p sun 2 - 7p

opened in 2007. owner: philippe alvergne
all major credit cards accepted

3rd arr > **s42**

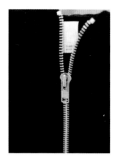

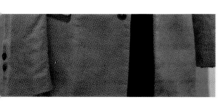

It is easy to fantasize about what life could be like but never make the changes. I've certainly said, "Oh, I'll do that when I'm older." Call me Tony Robbins, but today is the first day of the rest of my life! And I am going to wear nicer clothes. First stop: *Tremblay Alvergne*. This Paris-based designer makes clothes that would make the strictest of lifestyle coaches take notice. Made of wool and cashmere, knit tops and blazers are tailored—a bit preppy but hip, and not at all country club. With my new look pulled together, I'm ready to start my inspirational lecture series soon at a Holiday Inn near you.

covet:
tremblay alvergne:
 harris tweed jacket
 jersey cotton shirts
 wool, cotton & cashmere cardigan
 corduroy button-down shirt
 cotton moleskin pants
 wool, cotton & cashmere zippered pullover
 alpaca & cotton cardigan

zut!

refurbished industrial antiques, specifically clocks
9 rue ravignan. between rue des trois fréres and rue des abbesses
metro 12: abbesses
33 (0) 1 42 59 69 68 www.antiquites-industrielles.com
wed - sat 11a - 1p, 4 - 7p or by appointment

opened in 2001. owner: frederic daniel
cash only
online shopping

18th arr > **s43**

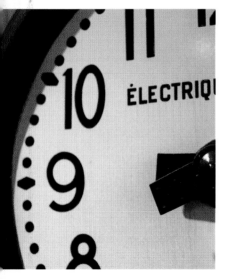

A pox upon you, Atlantic Ocean! Because of your hugeness, I am unable to carry home many things I desperately desire. For example, If *Zut!* were in Kansas City, I would have no reservations buying one of their amazing, refurbished train station clocks and driving it home. But the silly ocean makes that plan impossible. I guess I could buy a boat, learn to drive it and bring the clock home via the Panama Canal. It would be worth it to have some of these cool vintage items. I guess though I'll accept reality and fly home with more modest souvenirs tucked in my carry-on bag as I curse the big blue Atlantic below.

covet:
railway enameled ato clocks
double faced lepaute clocks
'40s singer stool
jean prouvé work chair
gras de marbrier lamp
veterinary school pig model
vulcanized cardboard box
eight foot tall welded eiffel tower

notes

etc.

the eat.shop guides were created by kaie wellman and are published by cabazon books

eat.shop paris 2nd edition was written, researched and photographed by jon hart

editing: kaie wellman   copy editing: lynn king   fact checking: michaela cotter santen
map and layout production: julia dickey and bryan wolf

jon thx: jodi and patrick for their help and lars for his stellar apartment

cabazon books: eat.shop paris 2nd edition
ISBN-13 9780982325445

the eat.shop guides are distributed by independent publishers group: www.ipgbook.com

to peer further into the world of eat.shop and to buy books, please visit: www.eatshopguides.com